The Black Rise:

Empowering Black Entrepreneurs to Elevate Their Businesses

By: The B.L.A.C.K. Masterminds

ISBN: 979-8-9883402-0-1

Printed in USA

Publisher: Backhouse Publishing

Table of Contents

Dedication

This book is dedicated to all the Black entrepreneurs who have faced systemic barriers and discrimination but refused to give up on their dreams. Your resilience, creativity, and determination inspire us all. We hope that this book will serve as a guide and inspiration for you to continue breaking chains and building successful businesses that make a positive impact in your communities and beyond.

Foreword

In a world where dreams can sometimes seem elusive, there are those who rise above adversity, break free from societal limitations, and carve their own path to success. Historically, Black communities have shown remarkable entrepreneurial spirit and resilience, exemplified by the thriving Black Wall Street communities of the past. *The Black Rise* stands as a beacon of hope, a blueprint designed to empower, educate, and inspire individuals on the remarkable journey of becoming a successful Black entrepreneur.

Within these pages, you will find a tapestry of stories, wisdom, and practical insights that illuminate the paths taken by those who have triumphed against all odds. The entrepreneurial landscape is often challenging for anyone, but for Black entrepreneurs, unique obstacles must be overcome. Systemic barriers, limited access to resources, and ingrained biases can test resilience and dampen the flames of ambition. Yet, throughout history, Black entrepreneurs have emerged as beacons of inspiration, proving time and again that greatness knows no bounds.

The Black Rise serves as a comprehensive roadmap for navigating the entrepreneurial terrain. From the initial spark of an idea to the execution of a successful venture, each chapter is imbued with the wisdom of those who have walked this path before.

The pages of this book introduce visionaries who have shattered glass ceilings, innovators who have disrupted industries, and trailblazers who have rewritten the narrative. As you immerse yourself in these narratives, you will find practical strategies and actionable advice to help you overcome obstacles and maximize your potential. From developing a strong personal brand to building resilient networks and formulating strategies, you will discover a treasure trove of insights that will fuel your entrepreneurial spirit.

The Black Rise is not solely a roadmap for personal success; it is also a call to action. It beckons us to challenge the status quo, shatter stereotypes, and foster an inclusive entrepreneurial ecosystem where Black business owners can thrive. It encompasses methodologies and serves as an affirmation that untapped potential lies dormant within Black communities.

To the aspiring Black entrepreneurs who hold this book in their hands, I implore you to let its contents ignite the flames of ambition within you. Let it be a compass that guides you through uncharted territories. But above all, let it be a reminder that the power to create change lies within you.

Success is not guaranteed, *The Black Rise* is a testament to the fact that greatness can be achieved by those who dare to dream, persevere through adversity, and embrace the possibilities that lie ahead. The path may be arduous, but it is in your hands to redefine what is possible and pave the way for generations to come.

As you delve into the depths of this book, you will learn the art of harnessing your unique strengths, leveraging your cultural heritage, and embracing the diversity that lies at the heart of your entrepreneurial journey. You will discover the power of resilience, adaptability, and perseverance in the face of challenges that may arise along the way.

As an advisor of The B.L.A.C.K. Masterminds, I have witnessed their activism and the incredible work they have accomplished through Black business collaborations. The B.L.A.C.K. Masterminds have been recognized for their efforts and selected as a recipient of the Nonprofit Tech Acceleration (NTA) program, made available through Microsoft's Racial Equity Initiative. Their dedication also earned them an invitation to attend a Black History symposium, featuring Black-led organizations led by TechSoup, a non-profit organization providing technology solutions and support to non-profits worldwide. The momentum continues to grow as they host their annual "Black Friday Takeover," a twenty-four-hour marathon of education, inspiration, and fun, where speakers from diverse genres share their experiences and business strategies.

The Black Rise will be an effective tool for those who seek success. It is a reminder that success is not an entitlement but the product of relentless passion, unwavering dedication, and unyielding determination. This book is a testament to the fact that Black entrepreneurs possess all the essential ingredients to thrive and reshape the business landscape. It serves as a reminder that you are not alone on this journey—countless Black entrepreneurs have walked this path before you, and their stories serve as beacons of hope and inspiration.

Trena Easley Armstrong, M.A.

Historian-Researcher

Introduction

The journey of entrepreneurship is a challenging path, filled with obstacles and hurdles that test the determination and resilience of any aspiring business owner. However, for Black entrepreneurs, this journey often becomes even more arduous due to systemic barriers and discrimination they face. In part one, "Dissecting the Black Lie," we aim to debunk the myths that have held back Black entrepreneurs and provide insights into the key factors necessary for success.

Part 1 of this book serves as the foundation for the rest of the journey, offering practical advice and strategies to level up your skills, leverage connections, break free from chains of limitation, and develop a boss mentality. We believe that by empowering Black entrepreneurs with these essential tools, they can begin to dismantle the barriers that impede their progress.

In Part 2, we delve into the concept of the urban revolution and how Black entrepreneurs can rewrite the rules to create thriving businesses. We explore the importance of designing the ultimate business blueprint and emphasize the significance of strategic thinking over tactical maneuvers. By embracing innovative strategies, Black entrepreneurs can reshape their approach to business and unlock new avenues for success.

Part 3 takes a deep dive into the process of building a successful Black-owned business. We provide a comprehensive, step-by-step guide to mastering the Rise Up Business Blueprint. This includes creating a business success plan, defining a core purpose that aligns with your values, setting bold and innovative goals, establishing a dynamic organizational structure, leading with impact, cultivating a winning team, discovering the art of branding and marketing, and streamlining business operations with smart systems.

In the epilogue, we reignite the dream for Black-owned businesses and inspire aspiring entrepreneurs to take action. We acknowledge the challenges faced by Black entrepreneurs but also highlight the immense potential and resilience within their communities. With this book, we aspire to serve as a guide and a source of inspiration, providing Black entrepreneurs with the tools and motivation they need to overcome obstacles and achieve their dreams.

By empowering Black entrepreneurs, dismantling barriers, and fostering a supportive ecosystem, we believe we can create a future where Black-owned businesses flourish and contribute significantly to the economic and social landscape.

Part 1: Dissecting the Black Lie

CHAPTER 1
Debunking the Black Lie

The Black lie is a myth that has held our community back for far too long, and it's time to shatter it once and for all.

The Black lie is the belief that Black people are not good business owners, that Black businesses are short-lived, inconsistent, and do poorly at customer service. But we're here to tell you this couldn't be further from the truth. There are countless examples of successful Black entrepreneurs and businesses, like Richelieu Dennis, the founder of Shea Moisture, who defied these stereotypes and prove that Black businesses can thrive.

But let's be honest, being a successful entrepreneur is not easy, and it's not just about having a great idea or a lot of passion. It takes hard work, dedication, and a willingness to learn from your mistakes. It takes the skills and knowledge to turn your idea into a successful business.

So, how do we break free from the Black lie and empower ourselves to elevate our businesses? First, we need to focus on building our skills and knowledge. This means investing in ourselves through education, training, and mentorship. We need to learn everything we can about our industry, our target market, and the latest trends and technologies. One of the ways we collectively do this is through our B.L.A.C.K. Friday Takeover. BLACK is an acronym for Building Leaders and Activating Collective

Knowledge. While it is only a one-day event, the conversations, connections, and lessons learned are timeless and extend past the 24 hours. Separately, each one of us practices what we preach and invests in our personal development and our businesses, including enrolling in courses for coaching, tools, and more. Curtis, our treasurer, is known for investing in exclusive coaching programs for professionals. Caliph, our Vice President, has a reputation for having his ear to the ground on all things vegan and social media. Our President Rhonda's passion for art is evident in her large collection of tools, paint, supplies, etc. LaCheka our secretary, stays active in the nonprofit sector investing in sector learning, networking and technology.

Second, we need to be willing to put in the hard work and make the sacrifices necessary to succeed. Building a successful business is not a sprint; it's a marathon. It takes time, effort, and a lot of drive. But if we're willing to put in the work, we can achieve our goals and make our dreams a reality.

Finally, we need to remember that we're not alone. We have a community of fellow Black entrepreneurs, community leaders, and influencers who are facing the same challenges and opportunities as we are. We can learn from each other, support each other, and build each other up.

Let's embrace our potential and reject the Black lie:

Black people are not good business owners, Black businesses are short-lived, Black businesses are not consistent, and Black businesses do poorly at customer service, do not network with other Black businesses, and don't pay well.

Let's focus on building our skills and knowledge, putting in the hard work, and supporting each other along the way. We have the power to create successful businesses and to make a difference in our communities. Let's seize this opportunity and rise to the top.

The Entrepreneurial Desire

We have countless examples of successful Black entrepreneurs and businesses, like Rodney Williams, the co-founder, and CEO of LISNR, who have defied these stereotypes and proven that Black businesses can thrive.

Now, let's talk about the entrepreneurial desire. This is the drive, the passion, and the obsession that takes over when you're struck with the idea of starting your own business. It's that feeling that you can't shake, that you need to break free and be your own boss. And if you're feeling that desire right now, we want you to know that you're not alone.

Take Rodney for example. Before he launched his company, he worked at Procter & Gamble (P&G) as a brand manager, working for someone else. But he was struck with that same urge, that same need to create something of his own. And now, he's the CEO of a successful technology company that uses ultrasonic data transmission to connect devices.

So, if you're feeling that same urge, don't let the Black lie hold you back. Don't let the myth of the heroic entrepreneur make you think that you have to be a rare breed to make it. You can do this. You have what it takes to start your own business and make it successful. If you have an existing business, the same applies to you – you have what it takes to catapult what you currently have. Just take that leap and believe in yourself.

And remember, starting a successful business is not just about having a great idea or a lot of passion. It takes hard work, dedication, and a willingness to learn from your mistakes. It takes the skills and knowledge to turn your idea into a successful business. So, invest in yourself through education, training, and mentorship. Learn everything you can about your industry, your target market, and the latest trends and technologies. And be willing to put in the hard work and make the sacrifices necessary to succeed.

The Fatal Assumption

Many people believe that just because they are an expert in a particular field, they automatically have the knowledge to run a successful business. But the truth is, running a business involves much more than expertise. It requires strategic planning, marketing, financial management, and more.

Let's give you an example of an African American entrepreneur, Tiffany, who started a hair salon business. She was a talented hairdresser, and her clients said she was so good that she should open her own salon. So, she did. But soon, Tiffany realized that running a business involved much more than styling hair. She had to manage employees, order supplies, market her business, and manage finances. Tiffany's dream had turned into a nightmare.

So, our advice to you is to gain a thorough understanding of all aspects of running a business. Attend workshops, read books, and seek advice from mentors with entrepreneurship experience. Remember, you're not just an expert; you're a business owner. With the right mindset and preparation, you can avoid the Black lie and build a successful business that allows you to live your dream.

With the advancements in technology, it's now easier to gain access to information, resources, and tools that can help you. Whether it's using social media to market your business or utilizing online accounting software to manage your finances, technology can be a powerful ally in building a successful business.

In conclusion, let's reject the Black lie and embrace the reality of what it takes to run a successful business. Let's focus on gaining a thorough understanding of all aspects of entrepreneurship, utilizing technology to our advantage. We have the power to create successful businesses and to make a difference in our communities.

CHAPTER 2
Identifying The Visionary, the Strategist, and the Expert

As prosperous visionaries, we've witnessed countless times that building a business is anything but simple. It's an intricate process demanding a distinct skill set and relentless effort. One of the most significant challenges many visionaries face is juggling the various roles they must fulfill in their business. You see, every visionary is essentially three personas in one: The Visionary, The Strategist, and The Expert. The reality is that each of these characters desires to be in charge, but no one wants to report to anyone. This creates conflict and may ultimately result in failure.

Let's break it down for you. The Visionary is the imaginative force, the big-picture thinker responsible for conceiving ideas and setting goals. The Strategist is the planner, devising systems and processes to ensure smooth operations. Lastly, The Expert is the doer, the one who completes the work and delivers products or services to customers.

Now, let's examine two personalities we can all relate to: The Cheerleader and The Hater. Ever gone on a diet? You start off strong, with The Cheerleader taking charge, but eventually, The Hater surfaces and sabotages your progress. This internal war also occurs within every small business owner.

The truth is each personality has its interests and methods. Asking any one of them to defer to another invites conflict or even all-out war. This is why it's vital for visionaries to comprehend these personality differences and learn to manage them effectively.

For instance, consider the rise of companies like Uber and Lyft. These businesses were established by visionaries with a plan to disrupt the transportation sector. However, their success wasn't solely due to their vision. They also had robust strategists who created the systems and processes needed to bring their vision to fruition. And, of course, they had experts who built the technology and delivered services to customers.

So, if you're a visionary, don't let the struggle between The Visionary, The Strategist, and The Expert hold you back. Instead, embrace all three personas and learn to manage them effectively. With the right mindset and approach, you can build a thriving business that makes a difference in the world.

The Visionary

The entrepreneurial spirit thrives within each of us. It's that spark, that drive, that propels us forward, transforming even the most ordinary circumstances into extraordinary opportunities.

As a visionary, you are the dreamer, the imagination igniting the fire of the future. You are the catalyst for change. You dwell in the future, never in the past, and seldom in the present. Your happiest moments are when you're free to imagine "what-if" and "if-when" scenarios.

In science, you witness the entrepreneurial personality at work in abstract, non-pragmatic areas like particle physics, pure mathematics, and theoretical astronomy. In art, it flourishes in the cutting-edge realm of the avant-garde. And in business, you are the innovator, the grand strategist, and the creator of new methods for penetrating or establishing new markets.

As a visionary, you are:

- The creative force that thrives when dealing with the unknown.
- Prodding the future.
- Turning possibilities into probabilities.
- Transforming chaos into harmony.

But let's be real; you also possess an extraordinary need for control. Living in the future, you require control over the present and the people and events around you, allowing you to focus on your dreams.

And yes, your need for change can create chaos, predictably unsettling those enlisted in your projects. But that's part of the game. As a result, you often find yourself rapidly outpacing others. The farther ahead you are, the greater the effort required to bring your team along.

So, how can you pursue opportunities without getting bogged down by obstacles? Well, the way you usually choose is to be persuasive, inspire, lead, and be relentless in chasing your dreams. You might have to step out of your comfort zone to make shit happen.

At the end of the day, you know that people can sometimes hinder your dream's progress. So stay focused, stay driven, and keep pushing forward. Remember, the entrepreneurial spirit is alive and well in every one of us. By tapping into that energy, drive, and creativity, there's nothing that can stop you from achieving your dreams.

The Strategist

The managerial personality is the backbone of any successful endeavor. The Strategist is the one who implements systems, creates structure, and ensures predictability in our businesses. They are the ones who take the vision of The Visionary and turn it into reality. For example, look at the successful tech company Square. The Visionary, Jack Dorsey, had the vision for a mobile payment system that would revolutionize transactions. But it was The Strategist, Jim McKelvey, who created the system and established the necessary infrastructure to make it a reality.

While The Visionary lives in the future, The Strategist dwells in the present, drawing on past experiences to create order and structure. Where The Visionary thrives on change and sees opportunity in every event, The Strategist seeks stability and perceives potential problems in every situation.

The Strategist is the one who keeps things running smoothly, ensuring that operations are efficient and effective. They create plans, set goals, and allocate resources to achieve success. The Strategist is critical to any business or organization, as they bring order out of chaos. However, it is the tension between The Visionary's vision and The Strategist's pragmatism that creates the perfect balance for success. Without The Visionary, there would be no innovation. Without The Strategist, there would be no structure or organization.

Take the example of successful African American visionary Richelieu Dennis. As the Visionary of Shea Moisture, he saw an opportunity to create natural hair and skin care products for people of color. However, it was The Strategist who helped grow the business by expanding product lines, developing new markets, and establishing a strong supply chain.

In conclusion, while The Visionary brings vision and creativity, The Strategist brings structure and organization. The synergy between the two creates the foundation for success.

The Expert

The Visionary dreams big, The Strategist lives in the past, but you, the Expert, live in the present. You love to tinker, and you know how to get things done. You understand that two tasks can't be completed simultaneously, so you work diligently, happiest when controlling the workflow.

However, you also question those you work for because they constantly try to accomplish more work than is either possible or necessary. You're not interested in lofty ideas or abstractions but in "how to do it." You know that all ideas must be translated into a methodology to have value.

The truth is that we all have a Visionary, Strategist, and Expert within us. If they were equally balanced, we'd be describing an incredibly competent individual. Unfortunately, experience shows that few people who go into business possess such balance. Instead, the typical small business owner is 10 percent Visionary, 20 percent Strategist, and 70 percent Expert.

If you find yourself in this situation, where you're in charge of your own business but spend most of your time doing technical work, then you need to reevaluate your priorities. Technical work for entrepreneurs encompasses the hands-on tasks and activities within their business, involving the application of specialized knowledge and skills to provide services or create products. Sure, you love doing hair or practicing your craft, but to be successful, you need to be more than just an Expert. You need to balance your Visionary, Strategist, and Expert personalities.

So, our advice is to embrace all three personalities and find the balance that works best for you. The Visionary wakes up with a vision, the Strategist solidifies the base of operations, and you, the Expert, do the technical work. Each derives satisfaction from the work they do best, serving the whole in the most productive way.

Remember, it's not just about doing the work. It's about doing the work that matters. Look at the B.L.A.C.K. Masterminds, for example. As successful visionaries and investors, we've adapted to changing times and embraced technology. We use social media to connect with our customers, invest in technology, and stay up to date with the latest trends in business.

So, whether you're a baker, fashion designer, or tech visionary, don't be afraid to learn new skills, embrace technology, and adapt to changing times. That's how you stay relevant and successful in today's world.

Now get out there, and make it happen!

CHAPTER 3
Leveling Up Your Skills

In the world of business, growth, and evolution are essential, just like in our own lives. Regrettably, far too many business owners operate their ventures based on personal preferences rather than what their businesses need. These experts yearn for a place to work free of limitations instead of embracing the roles of strategists and visionaries to propel their businesses forward.

Allow us to illustrate this with a relatable example: Joe, Tommy, and Mary are all business owners who experienced growth in their ventures but were unprepared for the challenges that came with it. Consumed by the hands-on aspects of their businesses, they struggled to carve out time for the strategic and managerial tasks necessary for elevating their businesses. Consequently, they found themselves working tirelessly, even on weekends, yet they continued to fall behind.

Now, don't get us wrong—there's absolutely nothing wrong with being an expert and enjoying the technical work. The problem arises when the expert personality dominates and neglects the other critical roles necessary for running a thriving business.

Being a phenomenal expert is simply not enough to build a remarkable small business. You must learn to balance hands-on work with strategic and managerial tasks. Embracing the visionary role is crucial for propelling your business forward and achieving success.

We understand that it can be challenging to envision your business operating without your direct involvement, but ponder this: if your customers choose your business based on your personality, presence, and expertise, what happens when you're not there? They will inevitably seek alternatives. Your focus should be on building a business that relies not only on your personal input but also on the systems, processes, and team you have in place.

Let's take a look at the success story of Tristan Walker, the founder of Walker & Company Brands, which includes Bevel—a grooming line specifically designed for Black men. As a visionary, Tristan recognized the need for better grooming products tailored to his community. However, it wasn't solely his vision that made the company successful. He surrounded himself with a skilled team and implemented solid strategies and systems that allowed the business to flourish and eventually be acquired by Procter & Gamble.

So, we challenge you to step up and assume the role of a leader in your business. Don't let the expert personality hold you back from achieving your dreams. Embrace the strategic and entrepreneurial roles and elevate your business to new heights.

Here are a few places where you can take free courses.

- Udemy- Udemy is a global marketplace for online learning and teaching. It offers over 155,000 courses in various subjects, including business, IT and software, personal development, design, marketing, and more. Udemy courses are created and taught by independent instructors from all over the world, and the platform provides tools for instructors to create and publish their courses. Students can take courses on-demand and at their own pace, and many courses offer certificates of completion.

- Coursera- Coursera is an online learning platform that partners with universities and organizations to offer courses, certificates, and degrees in various fields. It offers over 5,000 courses from top universities, including Stanford, Yale, and Columbia, as well as from organizations like Google and IBM. Coursera courses range from free to paid, and some courses offer certificates upon completion. Coursera also offers online degrees in fields like computer science, business, and data science.

- edX- edX is an online learning platform that offers courses and programs from top universities and organizations around the world. It was founded by Harvard University and MIT in 2012 and has since grown to include over 3,000 courses from over 150 institutions. edX courses are self-paced, and range from free to paid, and some courses offer certificates of completion. edX also offers micro-credentials, professional certificates, and online degrees in fields like engineering, computer science, and business.

- LinkedIn Learning is a comprehensive online platform with 155,000+ courses taught by global instructors. Subjects span business, IT, personal development, design, marketing, and more. Learn at your own pace, earn certificates, and access university partnerships for lifelong career growth.

Overall, these platforms are great resources for anyone looking to learn new skills or advance their career through online education. They offer a variety of courses and programs at different price points and many offer certificates and degrees that can help learners stand out in the job market.

In today's fast-paced world, being tech-savvy and well-informed about the latest industry trends is essential. Utilize social media platforms to connect with your customers, stay updated with innovative technology and practices, and never hesitate to learn new skills that will benefit your business.

Remember, the future belongs to those who dare to dream and have the courage to adapt. Be the change-maker your business needs and take charge of your destiny.

CHAPTER 4

Leveraging Connections: Your Network is Your Net Worth

Let us emphasize the significance of a pivotal moment in every business's journey—the moment you decide to hire your first employee or contractor. This marks the beginning of your business's adolescence, and it's always precipitated by a crisis in its infancy stage. As a small business owner, you're all too familiar with the overwhelming feeling of juggling countless tasks. That's precisely why seeking assistance becomes an inevitable necessity, and the help you require is technical.

For example, if you excel in sales, you'll need a production expert. Conversely, if you're production-oriented, you'll need a sales specialist. And nearly everyone requires someone to manage their finances. But how do you identify the right individual for the job? You need someone with experience, someone who understands your type of business and can execute the technical work you don't enjoy doing.

Imagine you find Malcolm—a 68-year-old bookkeeper who's spent 22 years mastering the books for a company strikingly similar to yours. Malcolm is proficient in handling the books in eight different languages and boasts an extensive experience that surpasses your wildest expectations. He's the ideal candidate to manage your business's financial side, and now he's on your team.

When Monday morning arrives, you greet Malcolm with enthusiasm, knowing your life is about to become more manageable. You've prepared a space for him,, organized the books and unopened letters on his desk, and even purchased a personalized coffee mug just for him.

Malcolm's arrival signifies a turning point for your business. With him handling the financial aspects, you can concentrate on other facets of your venture. However, be cautious not to fall into the trap of management by abdication, in which you hand over everything to Malcolm and flee.

With Malcolm's assistance, you can answer phone calls, manage shipping and receiving tasks, and even attend to a few customers. As your business expands, Malcolm recruits more team members, and life becomes increasingly easier. You get to be the strategist, focusing on the work you love, while Malcolm takes care of the rest.

But here's the catch—you can't afford to neglect Malcolm. Delegate, don't abdicate. Stay informed about his progress and the work he's doing. If problems arise, take responsibility and address them.

Take a cue again from the creator of Shae Moisture, Richelieu Dennis, who also founded Sundial Brands and Nubian Heritage. Richelieu understood the importance of leveraging connections and building a strong team that complemented his skills. His dedication to his vision, combined with the support of a well-rounded team, led Sundial Brands to become one of the fastest-growing African-American-owned companies in the United States.

Hiring your first employee or contractor is a critical milestone in your business's evolution. It's an indication that your business is maturing, and it's time for you to focus on being the strategist. Take that leap and hire that first employee or contractor. Your business will undoubtedly thank you for it!

CHAPTER 5
Breaking Chains

Every thriving business encounters a pivotal phase where it extends beyond the founder's comfort zone. This essential juncture demands a crucial decision – elevate your entrepreneurial game or risk your business spiraling out of control.

You must recognize that your capacity to shape your surroundings has its limits. As a visionary, you're restrained by what you can achieve independently. As a manager, your constraints are defined by the number of visionaries you can effectively oversee or the number of subordinate managers you can coordinate into a fruitful endeavor. However, as an entrepreneur, your boundaries are dictated by the number of managers you can inspire to pursue your vision.

Reflect on Damon John's company FUBU, for a moment. FUBU stands for, For Us By Us, and was a pioneering fashion brand in the 90s that represented empowerment, diversity, and urban style. Initially, it was merely Damon and a group of friends selling hats on the streets. But as they expanded, they acknowledged that they couldn't singlehandedly manage everything. They needed assistance, so they brought in a skilled manager to supervise the visionaries and help materialize their vision.

As your business scales, you'll inevitably reach a point where you can no longer be intimately involved in every task that demands attention. Focusing on familiar territory instead of venturing into the unknown is tempting, but that's where the peril lurks. You'll find yourself passing your responsibilities onto someone else, a "Malcolm," in the hopes that they'll take care of it, alleviating your concerns.

However, the reality is that Malcolm requires more than mere instruction. He needs to comprehend the purpose behind his actions, the outcomes for which he's responsible, and the criteria by which his work is assessed. Additionally, he must understand the trajectory of the business and how his responsibilities align with the overarching strategy.

For Malcolm to perform effectively, he needs something you, a visionary-turned-business-owner, might struggle to provide—a proficient manager! The absence of one can send a business into a downward spiral.

So, when your business outgrows your comfort zone and begins to falter, you have three potential paths:

First, revert to the beginning. Start anew, applying the invaluable lessons you've acquired throughout your journey.

Second, go all in. Embrace significant risks with the potential for substantial rewards. But beware, this high-stakes approach can have dire consequences if not executed judiciously.

Lastly, hold on tight. Persist in your current activities but acknowledge that the landscape has irrevocably changed.

Entrepreneurs heed our advice as a prosperous business owners:

- Invest in a competent manager or system to elevate your enterprise. The prospect might be daunting, but it's the only surefire method to prevent your business from spiraling into chaos.

- Embrace this approach, and you'll find yourself on a trajectory toward greatness – one that mirrors the successful paths of contemporary entrepreneurs like Elon Musk with SpaceX and Tesla or Sara Blakely with Spanx.

- Learn from their experiences, adapt, and propel your business forward in today's rapidly evolving, technologically driven world.

THE ART OF EMBRACING EXPANSION

Let's delve into the vital evolution from a Visionary to a proficient Expert in the dynamic and ever-changing landscape of business and technology. It's important to note that the Visionary holds the initial vision, while the Strategist establishes the foundation for operations. As the Expert, you will bring to life the technical work, driving the vision forward and making it a reality.

We all begin our entrepreneurial journey with a vision for our business. We're strategists at heart, handling every aspect of our operations because we believe we know best. However, as our businesses expand, so does the chaos. We may feel overwhelmed, even drowning in the responsibilities that growth brings. The temptation to revert to a smaller, more manageable state is strong. But is that truly the answer?

Remember Blockbuster? We can take a page out of their book. They were once reigning over the video rental industry. They first stumbled when faced with Redbox, then later, Netflix's disruptive innovation. Instead of adapting, they shrank. They closed stores, laid off employees, and tried to return to their former glory days. The result? Bankruptcy.

Don't let the same fate befall your business. Reverting to a smaller state isn't a viable long-term solution. It results in owning a job, not a business. Ultimately, your doors will close, and you will be miserable.

There's a better way. Recognize when it's time to shift gears from visionary to expert. This means relinquishing control and delegating tasks to skilled individuals who can help you achieve your vision. Develop a strategic plan and maintain a clear understanding of your goals.

Oprah Winfrey offers an inspiring example. Beginning as a television host, she aspired to do more. She embraced her entrepreneurial spirit, founded her own production company, and eventually launched her television network, and later, a media conglomerate. Rather than shrinking when faced with challenges, she persevered and made calculated moves to realize her dreams.

Don't fall into the trap of "going small." Embrace the chaos, recognize when it's time to pivot and forge ahead toward your vision. You can achieve success beyond your wildest dreams through hard work and determination.

MASTERING THE TECH FRONTIER

In the high-stakes realm of technology, many passionate visionaries launch businesses centered around the products they create, often neglecting the broader business landscape. While the excitement of innovative technology and a hungry market can be intoxicating, this approach can spell disaster.

In our fast-paced tech world, it's crucial to step back and gain perspective on your business. Excesses that might be manageable in a moderately growing company can be catastrophic in a high-speed, high-stakes environment.

You may believe that luck, speed, and innovative technology are all you need to succeed. But the truth is, there's always someone luckier, faster, and more technologically advanced. Once you're racing ahead, there's little time to pause and reflect.

We implore you to sidestep the high-tech game of Russian Roulette. Don't gamble with a game where you're uncertain if the gun is loaded.

Instead, concentrate on establishing a robust business foundation. Understand your market and customers and stay ahead of the competition. Learn from successful companies like Netflix, Amazon, and Apple. They didn't rely solely on groundbreaking technology or products; they built a brand, a culture, and a loyal customer base.

Success encompasses more than the product; it's about the process. As a community of entrepreneurs, let's forge a future where we all triumph together.

EMBRACING ENTREPRENEURIAL GROWTH

As an entrepreneur, particularly an African American entrepreneur, your dedication and determination to your business are undeniably inspiring. However, the key to lasting success doesn't solely lie in your commitment to always being present. Striking the right balance is crucial to avoid burnout and foster growth. By learning from the stories of fellow entrepreneurs, leveraging technology, delegating effectively, and seeking a supportive community, you can propel your business beyond the challenges of adolescence and into maturity.

Take a look at the journey of James, a talented baker and entrepreneur who invested his heart and soul into his thriving bakery. He believed that his constant presence was the secret to his business's success. However, when his right-hand employee, Michael, left the company, James found himself overwhelmed and couldn't trust anyone else to fill the void. His relentless pursuit of control ultimately led to his business's downfall.

This story is far too familiar for many entrepreneurs. Thankfully, the right tools, strategies, and support can help you avoid these pitfalls and attain lasting success. Let's explore some key approaches that can keep your business on the path to greatness.

- Harnessing Technology: Implementing the latest digital tools can help you streamline operations, automate tasks, and manage employees more effectively. For example, online scheduling tools assist in managing employees' schedules, project management tools keep you updated on tasks and deadlines, and inventory management tools ensure optimal stock levels.

- Delegating Effectively: As an entrepreneur, mastering the art of delegation is essential. Identify trustworthy employees, delegate tasks outside your strengths, and provide clear instructions. Effective delegation not only prevents burnout but also allows you to concentrate on tasks that require your unique touch.

- Building a Support Network: Surround yourself with a community that offers guidance, resources, and advice. Take for instance peer to peer networking groups, online communities, industry brand conferences and gatherings and mastermind groups.

By leveraging technology, delegating tasks effectively, and seeking support, you can build a successful company that positively impacts the lives of many.

As an entrepreneur, you're continually faced with chaos and challenges. Your response to these trials will determine your success. Embrace the chaos as an opportunity for growth rather than allowing it to consume you. Equip yourself and your business to flourish by understanding your key processes, asking the right questions, and crafting a visionary plan for the future. Remember that any plan is better than no plan, and the process of defining your future will shape your reality.

The growth of your business is in your hands. By dictating its pace and direction, you can create a company that not only supports you and your family but also empowers and improves the lives of others. Create your unique path, fueled by your passion and entrepreneurial spirit, and watch your business evolve into a lasting success story that inspires generations to come.

CHAPTER 6
Developing the Boss Mentality

The Entrepreneurial Perspective: A Modern Approach to Business Maturity for Black Entrepreneurs

Maturity, the often overlooked phase of a company's growth, is crucial for success. African American entrepreneurs can draw inspiration from visionary leaders who understood that maturity requires conscious effort from the beginning. By adopting a unique perspective on business and leveraging modern technology, entrepreneurs can create thriving ventures.

The Entrepreneurial Perspective: Lessons from IBM's Founder

A story about Tom Watson, the founder of IBM, sheds light on the importance of the entrepreneurial perspective. He attributed IBM's phenomenal success to three factors: a clear picture of the finished company, an understanding of how the company should act, and the realization that it needed to act like a great company from the very beginning.

Despite IBM's challenges, the takeaway from Watson's story is the significance of perspective. His vision for IBM and his insistence on adopting a mature outlook from the onset offer invaluable lessons for entrepreneurs, particularly those within the African American community, on the critical importance of starting with an entrepreneurial perspective.

In today's rapidly evolving business landscape, the right perspective is crucial. The entrepreneurial perspective involves having a clear vision of the future, understanding how your business should behave, and constantly aligning your actions with that vision. This perspective applies to all businesses, from large corporations to small startups and individual entrepreneurs, regardless of size.

Cultivating the Entrepreneurial Perspective

- Develop a clear vision: Before launching your business, or brand campaign, product etc., create a detailed mental picture of your fully mature company or idea. Consider the products or services you'll offer, the organizational structure, and your target customers. A clear vision enables you to make informed decisions as your business grows.

- Understand your business's ideal behavior: Reflect on how your mature company will need to act to achieve its goals. What type of culture should you cultivate? What kind of customer service will you provide? How will you market your products or services? By understanding your business's ideal behavior, you can begin acting accordingly from day one.

- Continually assess progress: Regularly evaluate your progress toward your vision. Identify any discrepancies between your current and ideal actions, and work to close those gaps. Ongoing progress evaluation allows for adjustments and improvements that keep you on track toward your vision.

- Learn from others: Draw inspiration and guidance from successful entrepreneurs and companies. Study their approach to business and how they maintain an entrepreneurial perspective. Apply their lessons to your own business by learning from their successes and failures.

- Be adaptable: The business world is in constant flux. To succeed, you must be flexible and adaptable. Remain open to new ideas and opportunities and be willing to change course if it brings you closer to your vision.

Embracing the entrepreneurial perspective enables African American entrepreneurs and all entrepreneurs to build successful, mature businesses capable of weathering the challenges of the modern business world and world events like a pandemic. This perspective is not only essential for business success but also serves as a powerful tool for personal growth and development.

As you embark on your entrepreneurial journey, remember the importance of adopting the right perspective. Keep your vision in mind, behave like the mature company you aspire to become, and consistently work toward your goals. By doing so, you'll be well on your way to building a successful, mature business that will stand the test of time, debunking the myth that Black businesses are short-lived. By incorporating the entrepreneurial perspective into your daily operations, you'll not only lay the foundation for a thriving business but also inspire the next generation of African American entrepreneurs and contribute to a more diverse and innovative business landscape. Success starts with perspective, and with the right mindset, you can transform your vision into a reality that lasts.

Part 2: The Urban Revolution: Rewriting the Rules for Black Entrepreneurs

CHAPTER 7
Embracing the Urban Revolution

The Digital Revolution, the Technological Transformation, and the Information Surge are all well-known occurrences in today's world. Their profound impact on our lives is undeniable.

However, when it comes to the Urban Revolution, many people might be left puzzled. Yet, the significance of the Urban Revolution on American small businesses and the insights we can glean for the future are as far-reaching as any of the previously mentioned phenomena.

At the core of the Urban Revolution lies a business approach with the potential to radically change any small business—or any enterprise, regardless of size—from a state of disarray and stagnation to one of order, enthusiasm, and constant growth. It is the Urban Revolution that equips us with the elusive key to crafting an exceptional business: the ultimate balanced model of a thriving enterprise.

The Franchise Phenomenon

It all began in 1992 when a young entrepreneur named James Lindsay opened the first Black-owned franchise of the popular restaurant chain, Checkers, in Miami, Florida. Through hard work, dedication, and a keen understanding of the business model, Lindsay was able to expand his empire to include multiple locations across South Florida.

Lindsay's success demonstrates the power of the Urban Revolution, as he took a well-established franchise model and tailored it to suit his target audience. By doing so, he not only tapped into a profitable market but also contributed to the growth of Black entrepreneurship and wealth.

Today, Black-owned franchises like Slutty Vegan, owned by Pinky Cole, have continued to thrive by blending innovative business strategies with a strong commitment to community engagement. Slutty Vegan has managed to create a buzz around plant-based food and has become a staple in the Atlanta food scene since its inception in 2018. The brand has expanded rapidly, with multiple locations and a food truck, serving as an inspiration for Black entrepreneurs everywhere.

"The Most Successful Small Businesses in America"

That's what these Black-owned franchises aspire to be called today. And with good reason, as their achievements are truly impressive.

When you consider how Slutty Vegan has grown in relatively short periods, it becomes clear that these entrepreneurs have embraced the Urban Revolution and harnessed its power to create thriving businesses. By adopting proven franchise models and adapting them to resonate with their target audiences, they've built the foundation for a new generation of entrepreneurs to follow.

These businesses, like their counterparts, have also been successful in creating employment opportunities, particularly for young people within their communities. This not only supports the economy but also empowers future generations of Black entrepreneurs.

The genius of these franchises lies not in the franchise model itself—which has been around for over a century—but in the Business Format Franchise. A business format franchise equips franchisees with a comprehensive toolkit, support, and expert guidance, empowering them to build and run their business under the trusted brand and high standards set by the franchisor. Many companies, such as Coca-Cola and General Motors, have leveraged franchising as an efficient distribution method for reaching expanding markets at a low cost. The true ingenuity of these businesses is their ability to embrace the Business Format Franchise and create scalable, replicable, and profitable business models.

According to more recent research, the success rate of franchises continues to outperform independently owned businesses. A study conducted by the International Franchise Association (IFA) in 2018 revealed that approximately 91% of franchise businesses were still operating after two years, indicating a significantly higher success rate compared to independent businesses. In contrast, the failure rate for independent businesses remains considerably higher, with various factors contributing to the challenges they face in achieving long-term sustainability. This stark comparison highlights the immense potential of the Urban Revolution in our economy and the substantial contribution that the Business Format Franchise has made—and will continue to make—to the future success of businesses, particularly for Black entrepreneurs. So, let us embrace the Urban Revolution and leverage its power to create thriving, lasting, and impactful businesses that inspire generations to come.

CHAPTER 8
Designing the Ultimate Business Blueprint

In the past, many franchise businesses operated as "trade name" franchises, some of which still exist today. Under this model, the franchisor licenses small companies to market its nationally recognized products on a local level. However, the modern franchise business model, known as the Business Format Franchise, goes beyond the trade name franchise.

The Business Format Franchise not only lends its name to smaller enterprises but also provides franchisees with a comprehensive system for conducting business. This key difference is what has driven the immense success of the Urban Revolution.

The Urban Revolution and the Business Format Franchise were established on a belief that counters the mindset of most business founders in the United States. Most founders believe that a business's success lies in the success of the product it sells. For trade name franchisors, the value of the franchise is in the brand name being licensed, such as Cadillac, Mercedes, or Coca-Cola.

While this belief may have held true in the past, it no longer does. As brand names multiply, establishing and maintaining a secure position with a brand name becomes increasingly difficult and expensive. Consequently, trade name franchises have declined as franchising, in general, has experienced unprecedented growth. The Business Format Franchise has driven this growth.

The Business Format Franchise is founded on the idea that the true product of a business is not what it sells but how it sells it. The real product of a business is the business itself.

Entrepreneurs like Janice Bryant Howroyd, the founder of ACT-1 Group, and Cathy Hughes, the founder of Urban One, have understood this principle. They realized that their businesses' true products were not their staffing services or media platforms but the businesses themselves.

These entrepreneurs shared a common challenge: having big dreams with limited resources. By embracing the franchise model, they found a way to achieve their aspirations. The franchisee became their vehicle to success. These entrepreneurs shifted their focus to perfecting their businesses and treating their franchisees as their most important customers.

Franchisees were not solely interested in the services or products being offered; they were interested in the business itself. They only wanted to know one thing: "Does it work?" These entrepreneurs then focused on ensuring that their businesses worked better than any other.

These businesses had to outperform not only their direct competitors but every other business opportunity available. Furthermore, they had to ensure that their businesses would work regardless of who bought them. In response to this challenge, these entrepreneurs created foolproof, predictable businesses that were systems-dependent rather than people-dependent. They worked on their businesses, not in them.

They started thinking about their businesses as engineers working on avatars for mass production. They re-engineered their businesses before the term, and the process became popular. They applied the principles of the Industrial Revolution to business development in a way that had never been done before.

The secret behind the Business Format Franchise and the Turn-Key Revolution is the Franchise Avatar. It is within the Franchise Avatar that successful franchisors build their future and plant the seeds of their fortune. It is also where entrepreneurs can find the model they need to make their businesses work.

For example, consider the founders of Slutty Vegan, Pinky Cole, and Miko's Italian Ice, Carmen Miko. These entrepreneurs have demonstrated the importance of the Franchise Avatar in creating successful businesses that cater to Black entrepreneurs and communities. Both have built their empires by focusing on how their businesses sell their products, not just the products themselves.

Slutty Vegan has been able to expand beyond its initial Atlanta location by providing its franchisees with a tried-and-true business model. Similarly, Miko's Italian Ice, which started as a small family-owned Italian ice stand in Chicago, has grown exponentially by offering its franchisees a proven system for success.

The Franchise Avatar addresses the following factors:

- Clear and consistent branding: Franchise businesses have developed strong brand identities that resonate with their target audience. This consistent branding helps ensure that every franchise location provides a similar customer experience, building trust and loyalty.

- Standardized operations: The Franchise Avatar involves a standardized set of operations that each franchisee must follow. This allows for efficiency, predictability, and uniformity across all locations, which benefits both the franchisor and franchisees.

- Comprehensive training and support: To ensure success, franchisors must provide franchisees with thorough training and ongoing support. This includes everything from initial training on company policies and procedures to ongoing guidance on marketing, management, and technology.

- Marketing and advertising: The franchise model relies on effective marketing strategies that promote brand awareness and drive business growth. Franchisors often provide marketing support to franchisees, including advertising campaigns, promotional materials, and guidance on local marketing efforts.

- Continuous improvement and innovation: Franchisors must stay ahead of industry trends and consumer preferences. By constantly seeking ways to improve products, services, and processes, franchisors can maintain a competitive edge and ensure long-term success for both themselves and their franchisees.

By following the principles of the Business Format Franchise, you can build thriving businesses that empower other entrepreneurs to achieve their dreams. The Turn-Key Revolution, driven by the modern franchise business model, has proven to be a game-changer in the world of business, providing opportunities for growth and success for countless individuals and communities.

In conclusion, the modern franchise business model has transformed the way businesses operate and expand. By focusing on how a business sells its products and services rather than just the products themselves, franchisors have created foolproof, systems-dependent businesses that are ripe for success. The Turn-Key Revolution has enabled entrepreneurs with limited resources to achieve their dreams by embracing the Business Format Franchise and the Franchise Avatar. This model has opened the door for successful, diverse businesses that cater to various communities, creating opportunities for growth and prosperity for both franchisors and franchisees alike.

CHAPTER 9

Elevate Your Business: Strategy Over Tactics

Here's the deal: your business isn't your life.

Your business and your life are two distinct entities.

Ideally, your business should be a separate entity from you, with its own set of rules and objectives. Think of it as an organism that thrives or fails based on its ability to fulfill its sole purpose: acquiring and retaining customers.

Once you understand that your life's purpose isn't to serve your business, but rather, your business's main objective is to serve your life, you'll be able to focus on working on your business, not just in it. That's when you'll truly understand the importance of this shift in mindset.

This is where you can leverage the Franchise Avatar model to your advantage.

Focusing on working on your business rather than in it will become the driving force behind your daily actions and the catalyst for everything you do moving forward.

Imagine that your current or future business serves as the avatar for 5,000 more identical establishments.

Your business is destined to become the blueprint for 5,000 other businesses, each one an exact replica. Perfect duplicates. Clones.

In other words, visualize your business as a franchise. (Note: We're suggesting you pretend, not that you actually should start a franchise. That's not the main takeaway here—unless, of course, that's what you want.)

Now, with the franchise mindset in place, you must understand that there are rules to follow if you want to come out on top:

- The model will consistently deliver exceptional value to customers, employees, suppliers, and lenders, surpassing their expectations.
- The model will be designed to be managed by individuals with the most basic skillset.
- The model will embody a space of impeccable organization and structure.
- All tasks within the model will be documented in comprehensive Operations Manuals.
- The model will guarantee a uniformly consistent customer experience.

- The model will adhere to branding standards such as a uniform color scheme, dress code, or facility standard.

Take, for instance, Rodney Williams, who saw an opportunity to revolutionize the way devices connect through sound. He recognized a gap in the market and developed a technology that enables seamless and secure data transmission using ultrasonic waves. His company has since become a leader in this field, with clients like Visa and Jaguar using his technology. Williams' success demonstrates how identifying a need and addressing it with a well-executed business model can lead to significant accomplishments. Black entrepreneurs can learn from his example by staying attuned to market trends and recognizing opportunities for innovation in their industries. Remember, it's important to understand that your business exists to serve your life, not the other way around.

As successful entrepreneurs, we've learned a few things about what it takes to build a thriving business. In this chapter, we want to share five critical rules that every entrepreneur should keep in mind if they want to build a business that will stand the test of time.

Rule 1: The Model Will Provide Consistent Value to Your Customers, Employees, Suppliers, and Lenders, Beyond What They Expect

Value is one of the most important concepts in business. It's what customers are looking for when they buy your product or service. But what is value, exactly? We define value as what people perceive it to be and nothing more.

As an entrepreneur, it's your job to create a business that provides consistent value to your customers, employees, suppliers, and lenders. But not just any value – value beyond their wildest expectations. This is the secret to building an extraordinary business.

So, how do you do this? One way is by going above and beyond in your customer service. For example, you could send a handwritten thank you note to every customer who makes a purchase or surprise them with a free gift in their order.

Another way is by making sure your product or service is of the highest quality. This means using the best materials, having the most knowledgeable staff, and constantly innovating to stay ahead of the competition.

Remember, value is essential to your business and to the satisfaction you get from it as it grows. It's not just about making money – it's about creating something that people truly love and appreciate.

Rule 2: The model will be operated by non-experts, and beginners.

This rule may sound counterintuitive, but it's crucial if you want to build a business that can grow and scale over time. Simply put, you need to create a system that doesn't rely on highly skilled people. Why? Because these people are expensive and hard to find.

Instead, you need to create a system that leverages the skills of ordinary people. This means creating processes and procedures that anyone can follow, regardless of their skill level. Of course, you still need to hire qualified staff – but you don't need to hire the best of the best for every role.

To do this, you need to focus on building a system that works. This means creating tools and processes that your staff can use to increase their productivity and get the job done in the way it needs to be done. By doing this, you'll be able to differentiate your business from the competition and create a consistent result for your customers.

Another benefit of this approach is that it makes it easier to manage your staff. When you have a system in place, you don't need to micromanage every employee. Instead, you can trust that they will follow the procedures you've created and produce the desired result.

Of course, this doesn't mean that people are unimportant. On the contrary, people are the ones who bring systems to life. But by creating a system that anyone can follow, you make it easier for your staff to do their jobs and produce the intended results.

Rule #3 is all about creating a place of impeccable order. In a world that's constantly in chaos, people crave structure and stability. With wars, famine, crime, violence, inflation, recession, and more all communicated instantly and continuously through the media, it's easy for people to feel a sense of powerlessness and pointlessness. The absence of structure can even lead to breakdown. Structure provides fixed points of reference that people need.

This is where an orderly business can come in. An orderly business can provide those fixed points of reference that people crave in a world of chaos. When your business looks orderly, it sends a message to your customers that your people know what they're doing. It also sends a message to your employees that you know what you're doing.

In a world that often doesn't work, an orderly business says that some things can be trusted. It assures your customers that they can trust in the result that you deliver and assures your employees that they can trust in their future with your company. When your business looks orderly, it says that the structure is in place, and people can rely on that structure.

Creating an orderly business is not just about appearances, however. It's also about creating systems and processes that are efficient and effective. It's about creating a workplace culture that values order and structure. This requires attention to detail, consistency, and a commitment to excellence.

For example, imagine a restaurant that looks immaculate. The tables are clean and set perfectly, the kitchen is spotless, and the servers are all dressed in clean uniforms. When customers come into the restaurant, they immediately feel that this is a place where they can trust the food and the service. They know that the kitchen is clean, the food is prepared with care, and the servers are attentive to their needs.

Now imagine the same restaurant but with dirty tables, a greasy kitchen, and servers dressed in stained and wrinkled uniforms. Customers would immediately feel uneasy about the quality of the food and the service. They might worry about the cleanliness of the kitchen and the possibility of food poisoning.

The same principles apply to any business. When you create an orderly workplace, you create an environment where people can trust the products or services that you provide. You create an environment where people can feel confident that you know what you're doing and that your employees know what they're doing.

But creating an orderly workplace is not just about creating a better customer experience. It's also about creating a better employee experience. When your workplace is orderly, your employees feel more productive, more focused, and more valued. They know that their work is important, and they know that they are part of a team that values order and structure.

An orderly workplace can also help to reduce stress and anxiety among employees. When there is a clear structure in place, and everyone knows their role and responsibilities, there is less confusion and uncertainty. This can help to create a more positive and supportive workplace culture where everyone feels that they are working towards a common goal.

Creating an orderly workplace requires attention to detail, consistency, and a commitment to excellence. It also requires a willingness to invest in the systems and processes that make your business run smoothly. This might include investing in training programs, technology, or other resources that can help to streamline your operations.

Rule #4 As an entrepreneur and business leader, we cannot stress enough the importance of documenting all the processes and procedures within your company. In other words, you need to have clear and concise Operations Manuals for every aspect of your business. This documentation serves as a guide for your employees, outlining the best practices, standards, and protocols for getting the job done in the most efficient and effective manner.

Think about it. Without documentation, all routinized work turns into exceptions. Your employees need structure, and that structure must be documented. This documentation reduces structure to specific means rather than generalized ends, which is necessary for the strategist in each of us to understand how to do the job at hand. The Operations Manual, which is essentially a How-to-Do-It Guide, is a repository of this documentation, outlining the purpose of the work, the necessary steps to take, and the standards to meet both during the process and the end result.

The key word here is clarity. Your people need clarity and structure to be productive and efficient. Without it, they are left to navigate the unknown, leading to inefficiencies, mistakes, and wasted time. Clear demands on your employees' time and energy provide an element of structure that they need to organize their lives and work. Documentation is an affirmation of order, providing structure, clarity, and predictability, all essential for a successful business.

Let us share a story that highlights the importance of predictability in the baking industry. We once visited a bakery that had the most delicious vegan doughnuts during our first visit. They were flaky, buttery, and had just the right amount of sweetness. The service was impeccable, and we left the bakery with a sense of satisfaction. We made a mental note to return to the bakery to purchase more doughnuts.

However, during subsequent visits, everything changed. The croissants were either over-baked or under-baked, the taste was inconsistent, and the service was lackluster. While the croissants were still decent, there was no consistency to the experience. The expectations created during the first visit were violated during subsequent visits, leaving us unsure of what to expect. We wanted a consistent experience that we could rely on when making the choice to return. The unpredictability deprived us of that experience, and it was ultimately the reason we chose not to return.

The unpredictability demonstrated that the baker was running the business for themselves, not for us, the customers. They had little sensitivity to the impact of their behavior on us and were depriving us of the experience of making a decision to patronize their business for our own reasons. It didn't matter what we wanted; what mattered was that the baker wasn't consistent with their service. It was as if they gave us a delightful experience and then took it away.

This is why consistency is critical in providing a uniformly predictable service to the customer. What you do in your model is not nearly as important as doing what you do the same way each and every time. This consistency builds trust and confidence in your brand, giving your customers the experience they expect and deserve. By providing predictability and consistency, you empower your customers to make informed decisions about your business, and you create an environment where they feel comfortable and secure.

Rule #5 Did you know that your business's colors and shapes can make or break your success? That's right! According to marketing studies, different consumer groups respond differently to specific colors and shapes. So, it's important to scientifically determine which colors and shapes work best for your business and then use them consistently throughout your model - on the walls, floors, ceiling, vehicles, invoices, people's clothes, displays, and signs.

Let's take the example of a clothing store. When a customer walks into your store, the color of the walls, the dressing rooms, and the clothes you're wearing can make all the difference in their shopping experience. But it's not just about the colors; it's also about the shapes. For instance, a circle could outperform a triangle in terms of sales, and a crest could outperform both!

Now, we know what you're thinking - "This all sounds great, but how can I possibly apply it to my business?" Well, it's all about packaging your business as carefully as any box of cereal. You need to think of your business as a world of its own, as a product of your efforts, as a machine designed to fulfill a very specific need, as a mechanism for giving you more life, and as a system of interconnecting parts. In short, think of it as anything but a job!

Once you change your perspective and start thinking about your business as a product, you'll be able to answer some important questions: How can I get my business to work without me? How can I get my people to work without my constant interference? How can I systematize my business in such a way that it could be replicated 5,000 times? And most importantly, how can I own my business and still be free of it?

But here's the thing - you can't do it alone. You need a process, a practice, by which to obtain specific information and a method with which to put that information to use productively.

Now, let's talk about some real-life examples of how Black entrepreneurs have successfully utilized the power of color, dress, and facilities code to take their businesses to the next level.

First up is Tracy Sanders, founder of the natural hair care brand, tgin (Thank God It's Natural). Sanders was inspired to start her business when she noticed a lack of affordable, quality natural hair care products for women of color. To stand out in a crowded market, Sanders made sure that her products were not only effective but also visually appealing. She utilized a color scheme of pastel green and pink, which not only looked good but also conveyed a message of health and wellness. Sanders also made sure that her brand's aesthetic was consistent across all touchpoints, from the product packaging to the website to the physical store. This consistency not only helped to establish tgin's brand identity but also made it easier for customers to recognize the brand and develop a sense of trust.

Another example is Marcellus Alexander, founder of Our Glass Media Group, a Black-owned multimedia company. Alexander recognized the importance of dressing for success and created a dress code for his team that reflected the company's professional image. Employees are required to dress in business attire, which includes suits, dress shoes, and ties for men and dresses, skirts, and blouses for women. This dress code not only helps to project a professional image but also serves as a reminder that they are representing the company at all times.

But it's not just about the dress code; facilities code also plays a crucial role in the success of a business. Take the example of Tierra Banks, founder of The Plus Academy, a plus-size modeling and etiquette school. Banks understood that the physical space of her business needed to reflect the values and mission of her brand. So, she made sure that her school was welcoming, comfortable, and inclusive for all body types. She utilized a warm color scheme of orange and yellow, which created a sense of energy and positivity, and incorporated features such as comfortable seating, mirrors, and adequate lighting to make the space feel inviting and conducive to learning.

In conclusion, the power of color, dress, and facilities code cannot be underestimated in the success of a business. As Black entrepreneurs, it's important that we utilize these tools to not only stand out in a crowded market but also to establish our brand identity, develop a sense of trust with our customers, and project a professional image. By packaging our businesses as carefully as any box of cereal and utilizing proven processes, we can take our businesses to the next level and achieve the success we deserve.

These rules may seem simple, but they are essential if you want to build a successful business. By providing consistent value to your customers, employees, suppliers, and lenders and by creating a system that leverages the skills of ordinary people, you'll be able to differentiate your business from the competition and create something truly extraordinary.

So, if you're an entrepreneur looking to build a business that will stand the test of time, keep these rules in mind. And remember, building a successful business is a journey – one that requires hard work, dedication, and a willingness to learn and adapt along the way.

Part 3: Building a Successful Black-Owned Business

CHAPTER 10

Mastering The Rise up Business Blueprint

Building the avatar of your business is just the beginning of an ongoing process that requires continuous innovation, quantification, and strategy. Each of these three distinct yet integrated activities are essential to the natural evolution of your business.

Let's talk about innovation, which is more than just being creative. It's about taking those creative ideas and turning them into reality. Black entrepreneurs like Rodney Williams of LISNR have demonstrated this by introducing disruptive technology that has revolutionized the way devices connect through sound. His company's ultrasonic data transmission technology has attracted clients like Visa and Jaguar and earned millions in funding.

Williams' innovation was driven by his desire to solve a real-world problem and create a solution that addresses it. By recognizing the need for more efficient and secure data transmission, Williams has created a technology that has disrupted the market and improved the lives of consumers. His success highlights the importance of identifying gaps in the market and developing innovative solutions to address them. As a Black entrepreneur, following Williams' example of innovation and a customer-centric approach can lead to success in any industry.

Quantification is all about measuring and analyzing key performance indicators (KPIs) to optimize performance. In today's tech-savvy world, Black entrepreneurs can use tools like "Blendoor" to quantify and analyze their business metrics. The app helps businesses track their diversity and inclusion efforts, providing valuable insights that can help improve performance and drive growth.

Finally, strategy involves creating systems and processes to streamline operations and improve efficiency. One example of this is "Afrocenchix," a Black-owned hair care company that has created a fully automated e-commerce platform. By using technology to automate their supply chain and order fulfillment processes, they have been able to reduce costs and improve customer satisfaction.

Remember, when it comes to innovation, it's not just about what you sell; it's about how you sell it. Take "Blavity," for example, a Black-owned media company that has found innovative ways to reach its audience. Through its online platform, events, and community-focused initiatives, Blavity has built a loyal following and become a leading voice in the Black community.

So, whether you're just starting out or looking to take your business to the next level, don't forget the importance of innovation, quantification, and strategy. By leveraging the latest technologies and best practices, you can build a successful business that meets the unique needs of your customers and drives growth.

*Instead of asking, "Hi, may I help you?" try "Hi, have you shopped with us before?" The customer will respond with either a "yes" or a "no." In either case, you're set to keep the conversation flowing.

If the answer is yes, you can say, "Awesome. We've designed an exclusive new program for our loyal customers. Let me take a minute to fill you in."

If the answer is no, you can say, "Fantastic, we've put together a special new program for first-time visitors. Let me take a minute to tell you about it."

Naturally, you'll need a unique new program to discuss. But that's a piece of cake.

Consider this: A few simple words. Nothing complex. But the outcome is sure to boost your revenue. How much? That relies on your level of enthusiasm. Our retail clients' experience shows that doing just this one thing can raise sales by 10 to 16 percent almost instantly!

Can you imagine? A few simple words and sales soar. Not just a tiny bit, but substantially! What would you do for a 10-to-16-percent bump in sales?

*Try this six-week experiment. For the first three weeks, wear a branded shirt, a pair of branded pants or skirt, and/or branded shoes. For the following three weeks, switch to a different branded shirt, a pair of branded pants or skirt, and/or branded shoes.

The outcome will be striking: sales will rise during the second three-week period! Why? Because, as our clients have consistently found, customers are more likely to purchase branded apparel and merchandise that is consistent with the company's image and messaging—regardless of who's wearing them.

Is it any surprise that trailblazing companies like Airbnb and many others invest so much in crafting their image? It pays off! And it does so consistently, time and time again.

To improve your customer interactions, for a brick & mortar, consider using non-verbal cues like a consistent smile, eye contact, and engagement to establish a connection with your customers. Research shows that non-verbal communication can be just as effective as verbal communication in building trust and rapport with customers.

As a business owner, you can encourage your sales team to practice these non-verbal communication techniques during customer interactions. For instance, instruct them to maintain eye contact, use a friendly tone or make a physical connection, such as a handshake.

By focusing on creating a positive and memorable experience for your customers, you can increase the likelihood of repeat business and positive word-of-mouth referrals. Incorporating non-verbal communication techniques can be an effective way to enhance your customer interactions and improve your sales outcomes.

Innovation lies at the core of every remarkable business. It continually asks: What's stopping my customer from getting what they want from my business?

For innovation to be impactful, it must always adopt the customer's perspective. Simultaneously, innovation streamlines your business to its essential elements. If it doesn't make things simpler for you and your team, it's not Innovation—it's complication.

Innovation, then, is the tool through which your business distinguishes itself in your customer's mind and establishes its uniqueness. It's the product of a scientifically crafted and quantifiably verified understanding of your customer's perceived needs and subconscious expectations.

It's the expertise cultivated within your business and your team that consistently asks, "What's the best way to do this?" knowing that, even as the question is posed, we may never find the best way—but by asking, we'll definitely find a better way than the one we know now.

In that sense, we see innovation as the "Best Way" skill. It generates a high level of energy in every company where it's nurtured, fueled, and stimulated—an energy that, in turn, invigorates everyone the company touches: its employees, customers, suppliers, and lenders. In an innovative company, everyone thrives.

There's no doubt about it: Innovation is the hallmark of a daring, creative spirit. It empowers entrepreneurs, especially Black entrepreneurs, by providing real-life, current examples of success that resonate with their unique experiences. By embracing innovation, businesses can create a lasting impact and inspire the next generation of trailblazers to forge their own paths to greatness.

Quantification

However, innovation alone won't get you far. For it to be effective, all innovations need to be quantified. Without Quantification, how would you know if the innovation worked?

By quantification, we're referring to measuring success; the numbers that indicate the impact an innovation makes.

For instance, ask any group of small business owners how many selling opportunities they had the day before, and we guarantee 99 percent of them won't know the answer.

Unfortunately, most businesses don't practice quantification, and it's costing them a fortune!

For example, how would you know that changing the words you use to greet customers resulted in a 16-percent increase in sales unless you quantified it by:

- Determining the number of people who entered before implementing the innovation.

- Determining the number of people who made purchases and the dollar value of those products before changing the words.

- Counting the number of people who entered after changing the words.

- Counting the number of people who made purchases.

- Calculating the average unit value of a sale.

- Determining the improvement as a result of your innovation.

These numbers enable you to gauge the exact value of your innovation.

How would you know that wearing a blue suit had a specific monetary impact on your business unless you quantified that impact and had a specific control against which to measure it? The answer is clear; you wouldn't.

As we've mentioned, few small business owners quantify these things, even those who believe in quantification.

Because few small business owners think that such seemingly trivial Innovations are really that important!

But ask yourself, if you could boost sales by 10 percent just by wearing a blue suit, would you do it? Would you make it a priority? The answer is as evident as the question is absurd. Of course, you would!

Quantification must address the obvious at the beginning of the Business Development Process.

Start by quantifying every aspect of your business operations. We mean everything. How many customers do you meet in person each day? How many in the morning? In the afternoon? Online?

How many calls/emails does your business receive daily? How many callers request a price? How many want to purchase something? How many units of product X are sold daily? At what time of day are they sold? How many are sold weekly? Which days are the busiest? How busy?

And so on.

You can't ask too many questions about the numbers.

In time, you and your team will view your entire business through the lens of numbers.

You'll quantify everything.

You'll be able to assess your business's health by analyzing the flow of the numbers.

You'll learn which numbers are crucial and which aren't.

You'll become as familiar with your business's numbers as your doctor is with your blood pressure and pulse rates.

Because without the numbers, you can't possibly know where you are, let alone where you're headed. With the numbers, your business will take on a whole new meaning.

It will brim with potential.

Strategy

The moment you innovate a process and measure its impact on your business, the moment you find something that works better than its predecessor, the moment you discover how to increase the "yeses" from your customers, employees, suppliers, and lenders - that's when it's time to orchestrate the entire operation.

Strategy is the process of eliminating discretion or choice at the operational level of your business.

Without strategy, nothing can be planned or anticipated - by you or your customers. If you're doing everything differently each time, if everyone in your company is doing it according to their discretion, their own choice, rather than creating order, you're creating chaos.

The rule of the day from the disciples of strategy is, "If 'Hi, have you been in here before?' works better than anything else you've tried, say it every single time you greet a customer."

By every disciple of strategy, we're referring to anyone who has ever seriously decided to produce a consistent, predictable result in the world of business, no matter their industry.

This includes black owned brands like Beauty Bakerie, a cosmetics brand founded by Cashmere Nicole, who also serves as the CEO. Another is The Honey Pot Company, a feminine hygiene and personal care brand founded by Beatrice Dixon. These companies and their CEOs are great examples of Black entrepreneurship and innovation in various industries.

Because every founder of every successful Business Format Franchise company, whether it's franchised or not, knows one thing to be true: if you haven't developed a strategy, you don't own it!

And if you don't own it, you can't rely on it.

And if you can't rely on it, you don't have a franchise.

And without a franchise, no business can hope to succeed.

And unless your unique way of doing business can be replicated every single time, you don't own it. You've lost it. And once you've lost it, you're out of business!

The need for strategy is based on the indisputable, quantifiable certainty that people will only do one thing predictably – be unpredictable.

But for your business to be predictable, your people must be. So, what's next? The system must provide the vehicle to facilitate predictability. To do what? To give your customers what they want every single time. Why? Because unless your customer gets everything they want every single time, they'll go elsewhere to get it!

Strategy is the glue that binds you to your customers' perceptions.

Strategy is the certainty that's absent from every other human experience. It's the order and logic behind the human craving for reason.

Strategy is as simple as doing what you do, saying what you say, looking the way you look—being who and how you are—for as long as it works, for as long as it produces the results you want.

And when it no longer works, change it! The Business Development Process isn't static. It's not something you do and then complete. It's something you do continuously.

In other words, once you've innovated, quantified, and orchestrated something in your business, you must continue to innovate, quantify, and orchestrate it.

The Business Development Process is dynamic because the world, with its constant motion, won't tolerate a stationary object.

The world will collide with whatever stands in its path. And if that stationary object happens to be your business, the results can be catastrophic.

So, you must continuously innovate, quantify, and strategize, never becoming complacent or resting on your laurels. This is the key to building a business that can stand the test of time, adapt to changing market conditions, and continue to deliver consistent, high-quality experiences for your customers.

Let's look at some examples of strategy in successful businesses:

- **Essence Communications, Inc.**
    - Industry: Media and Entertainment
    - Strategy: Essence Communications, Inc., the company behind Essence magazine, has focused on celebrating and empowering black women. By catering to a specific niche audience and understanding their unique needs, Essence has built a strong and loyal readership. The company has expanded its brand beyond the magazine, organizing events like the Essence Festival, which further solidifies its position as a leading media and entertainment brand in the African American community.
- **Roc Nation**
    - Industry: Entertainment and Sports Management
    - Strategy: Founded by rapper and entrepreneur Jay-Z, Roc Nation has emerged as a powerhouse in the entertainment and sports management industry. The company has embraced a diverse talent roster, representing artists, athletes, and even music

producers. Roc Nation's success lies in its ability to identify and nurture talent while providing them with a holistic approach to career management, encompassing branding, marketing, and strategic partnerships.

- **Pat McGrath Labs**
  - Industry: Cosmetics and Beauty
  - Strategy: Founded by renowned makeup artist Pat McGrath, Pat McGrath Labs has revolutionized the beauty industry. The brand has garnered a massive following by releasing limited-edition makeup collections that generate buzz and anticipation among beauty enthusiasts. By leveraging social media and influencer marketing, Pat McGrath Labs has created a sense of exclusivity and high demand for their products, leading to rapid growth and a cult-like following.

These examples demonstrate the power of strategy in creating a consistent, predictable experience for customers. By carefully controlling every aspect of your business, from product design to customer service, you can build a brand that stands out in a crowded marketplace and fosters loyalty among your customers.

In conclusion, the importance of strategy cannot be overstated. By eliminating discretion and choice at the operational level of your business, you can ensure that your customers receive the same high-quality experience every time they interact with your brand. This consistency is essential for building trust, loyalty, and, ultimately, a successful business. So, take the time to analyze every aspect of your operation, identify areas where you can introduce consistency and order, and then implement those changes to create a predictable, enjoyable experience for your customers.

By embracing the principles of innovation, quantification, and strategy, you can create a thriving business that is agile, adaptive, and poised for long-term success. Never stop refining and improving your processes; the world is constantly changing, and your business must evolve along with it. Stay focused on delivering exceptional value to your customers, and you'll build a brand that stands the test of time.

CHAPTER 11
Building Your Business Success Plan

You may have a great business idea, but how do you turn it into a model that can be replicated thousands of times? That's where the Franchise Avatar comes in.

Imagine this: a potential buyer walks through your door, and they're blown away by the order, predictability, and control in your business. They see that everything runs like a well-oiled machine, with innovative solutions to people's problems and quantifiable results. They want to buy your business, but only if it works without a lot of work and without you to work it.

To get there, you need a Business Development Plan, a step-by-step process that will turn your business into a perfectly organized model for thousands more just like it. Let's break it down into seven distinct steps:

Step 1: Your Primary Vision.

This is your long-term vision for your business. Where do you want to take it, and what impact do you want to have on the world?

Step 2: Your Strategic Plan.

This is your short-term plan to achieve your Primary Aim. What are your specific goals for the next year, and how will you measure success?

Step 3: Your Organizational Blueprint.

This is where you define the structure of your business, including your mission, values, and culture. How will you build a team that is aligned with your vision and can execute your plan?

Step 4: Your Management Map.

This is where you define how you will manage your team and resources to achieve your Strategic Objective. How will you delegate responsibilities, monitor progress, and make adjustments as needed?

Step 5: Your People Plan.

This is where you define how you will attract, develop, and retain top talent. What are your hiring criteria, training programs, and performance management systems?

Step 6: Your Marketing Strategy.

This is where you define how you will promote your business to your target audience. What channels will you use, and what message will you convey?

Step 7: Your Systems Strategy.

This is where you define how you will create and maintain systems that ensure consistency and quality in your products or services. How will you document your processes, measure your results, and improve your systems over time?

By following these steps, you can create a Franchise Avatar that can be replicated thousands of times and attract potential buyers impressed with your business's order, predictability, and control. And as a Black entrepreneur, you have unique experiences and perspectives that can give you an edge in the tech-savvy business world.

So, let's get started and turn your business into a model for success!

CHAPTER 12
Defining Your Core Purpose

It's time to talk about living with purpose and chasing your dreams with relentless passion. As Daymond John would say, "You've got to hustle, grind, and stay hungry to create the life you want." But first, you need to figure out your core values and define your ultimate goals. Your primary aim in life is the key to unlocking your full potential and achieving your dreams.

Picture your ideal future, the life you want to live, and the legacy you want to leave behind. That's your primary aim, and it should guide every decision you make. If you want to make a real impact, it's time to take control of your life and work with intention.

When it comes to business, particularly the tech industry, there are countless examples of Black entrepreneurs who have overcome challenges and built successful companies. These trailblazers prove that anyone can make it in the industry if they're willing to take risks, work hard, and follow their passions.

Take Brian Brackeen, an African American entrepreneur who founded Kairos, a facial recognition software company. Despite facing adversity and discrimination, he persevered and built a successful company that raised millions in funding. His determination and vision placed him at the forefront of innovation in the tech world.

Jewel Burks is another inspiring example of a Black entrepreneur who achieved greatness in the tech industry. She founded Partpic, a startup that uses visual recognition technology to streamline the industrial parts ordering process. After being acquired by Amazon, she went on to become the Head of Google for Startups in the U.S. Her story highlights the power of resilience and ambition in achieving success.

Again, Rodney Williams, is a great example of a Black entrepreneur who has made significant contributions to the tech industry. He created a new audio-based communication protocol that allows devices to communicate with each other using inaudible sound waves. This technology has numerous applications, from facilitating contactless payments to enhancing event experiences. Williams has secured millions in funding for his company and has received recognition as a Forbes 30 under 30 honoree, demonstrating that hard work and innovation can lead to remarkable achievements in the tech world.

And who could forget the incredible story of Kimberly Bryant, founder of Black Girls CODE? She started a non-profit organization to provide young Black girls with access to technology and computer programming education. Through her hard work and dedication, she's paving the way for a new generation of tech leaders and creating opportunities for countless young women.

Let these real-life examples inspire you to chase your dreams relentlessly. Keep hustling, keep grinding, and never lose sight of your primary aim. You can achieve anything if you believe in yourself and work hard for it.

Take a step back and ask yourself those crucial questions: What do you want your life to look like? How do you want to live your life on a day-to-day basis? What do you want to know about your life? How do you want to be with other people in your life? What do you want people to think about you? What do you want to be doing two years from now? Ten years from now? Twenty...

Let your primary vision guide you, and you'll be well on your way to living intentionally and creating a life you're proud of. Stay focused, stay hungry, and keep pushing forward. The world is waiting for your greatness.

As you work on your business and pursue your dreams, remember that you are part of a community of entrepreneurs who share your drive and determination. Lean on your network, build connections, and learn from those who have come before you. It's important to surround yourself with like-minded individuals who can support.

CHAPTER 13
Setting Bold and Innovative Goals

We all harbor grand dreams and aspirations for our lives, but it's essential to recognize that our businesses should be the catalyst propelling us toward those dreams, not an anchor weighing us down. This is where crafting a Strategic Plan becomes indispensable.

A Strategic Plan is a lucid declaration of what your business must accomplish to help you attain your Primary Vision in life. It envisions the final outcome your business will create. But let's be crystal clear - this isn't a business plan. It's born from the intersection of your Life Plan and your Business Strategy and Plan.

Your Life Plan should sculpt your life and the business that serves it. Meanwhile, your Business Strategy and Plan establish the framework for your business to evolve over time and fulfill your Life Plan. This approach communicates to everyone – from bankers and investors to strategic partners – the trajectory of your business and the specific milestones it needs to reach for success.

However, let's not get entangled in minutiae. Your strategic objective should comprise a set of straightforward and well-articulated benchmarks that help you gauge your progress toward your ultimate goal. It's a tool for execution, not justification. It's a blueprint for your business, ensuring that the time and energy you invest yield precisely what you desire.

For instance, consider the inspiring journey of Jessica Matthews, a successful African American entrepreneur and inventor. Her strategic objective was to harness the power of kinetic energy to create sustainable, affordable energy solutions. She created the SOCCKET, a soccer ball that generates electricity as it's kicked around and founded Uncharted Power, a company that develops innovative energy infrastructure solutions. Matthews has received numerous awards for her work, including recognition as a Forbes 30 under 30 honoree and a TED Talk speaker. Her dedication to using technology for social and environmental impact demonstrates how a clear objective can lead to remarkable achievements in entrepreneurship and innovation.

So, follow in the footsteps of trailblazing entrepreneurs like Jessica Matthews, and let your strategic plan be the guiding light to propel your business forward and bring your dreams to life.

First Strategic Plan: This crucial step will unlock your true potential and help you achieve the life you've always dreamed of.

Let's start by discussing the first standard of your Strategic Plan: money. We know it's not just about making a quick buck; it's about envisioning where you want your business to be. Are you building a $300,000 company, a million-dollar company, or a $500-million company? Set your sights on your financial goals so you can measure your success.

But let's get real - gross revenues alone won't do the trick. You need to understand your gross profits, pretax profits, after-tax profits, and more. Predicting sales years ahead might seem impossible, but any standards are better than no standards at the beginning of your business.

Create financial standards that align with your personal goals and the life you want to live. Consider not only income but also assets. How much money do you need to be truly free and independent?

Remember, the ultimate goal in creating a business is to sell it, just like Ray Kroc did with McDonald's. Craft a Franchise Avatar, a turn-key solution that outperforms the competition. By designing a reliable money-making machine, you'll attract prospective buyers who share your vision.

Once you've established financial standards, ensure your business has a realistic chance of achieving them.

Second Strategic Plan: Opportunity Worth Pursuing.

An Opportunity Worth Pursuing is a business that meets the financial standards you've set for your Primary Aim and Strategic Plan. If it can reasonably fulfill those standards, it's worth pursuing. Otherwise, no matter how enticing, it's best to move on.

To identify an Opportunity Worth Pursuing, ask yourself: Does the business I envision solve a problem or frustration for a large enough consumer base? If so, you're on the right track.

This standard satisfies two primary requirements of your Strategic Plan. It clarifies the type of business you're creating and defines your target customer. It tells you what to sell and to whom.

Now, let's differentiate between a commodity and a product. A commodity is a tangible item your customer takes home, while a product is the feeling your customer experiences after their purchase. Focus on the emotions your business evokes, not just the commodity.

Take Rihanna's Fenty Beauty as an example. The commodity is makeup, but the product is inclusivity and self-expression. Customers don't just buy makeup; they invest in the feelings of confidence and self-worth it provides.

Consider Nike's powerful ad campaigns. They don't just sell athletic gear (the commodity); they sell inspiration, motivation, and achievement (the product). By purchasing Nike products, customers believe they're part of something bigger.

Ask yourself, what feelings will customers associate with your business? Confidence? Security? Empowerment? Identify the emotions your customers crave and deliver them.

Keep in mind that people buy feelings, not just commodities. In today's complex world, the feelings we seek become more urgent and less rational. Your business's ability to anticipate and satisfy those feelings is your product. Cater to the demographics and psychographics of your target audience to achieve this.

Let's talk about one of the most crucial aspects of building a successful business: understanding your customers.

Every successful business has a Central Demographic Model or avatar, which is a set of defining characteristics that define their most probable customer. Demographics like age, sex, income, family status, education, and profession are essential to understanding your customer's motivations for buying or not buying from you. But it's not just about demographics; it's also about psychographics. Psychographics is the science of perceived marketplace reality, and it tells you why your customer buys. You need to know what emotional or perceived needs your customers have and how you can satisfy those needs.

For example, let's take the case of a successful Black-owned beauty brand called The Lip Bar. The Lip Bar's Central Demographic Model customer is women of color who prioritize inclusivity, simplicity, and self-expression. The Lip Bar satisfies their customers' emotional needs for inclusivity by offering a wide range of shades that flatter all skin tones and their commitment to creating products that are vegan and cruelty-free. Their simple and easy-to-use packaging reflects their commitment to creating makeup products that are accessible to everyone.

Another example is a Black-owned e-commerce company called Black Girl Magic Box. Black Girl Magic Box's Central Demographic Model customer is Black women who prioritize self-care, community, and supporting Black-owned businesses. Black Girl Magic Box satisfies their customers' emotional needs for self-care with their monthly subscription box that includes beauty, wellness, and lifestyle products from Black-owned businesses. Their commitment to supporting Black-owned businesses reflects their customers' values and priorities.

To create a successful business, you also need to set standards for your Strategic Plan. These standards shape both the future model of your business and the way it appears today. Start by asking yourself specific questions, such as when your avatar will be completed, where your business will be located, and how it will operate. What standards will you insist upon regarding reporting, cleanliness, clothing, management, hiring, firing, training, and so forth? These standards create the tension that draws your Strategic Plans closer to your current business reality.

For instance, let's look at Blavity. Blavity's Strategic Plan is to create a digital platform that amplifies Black voices, perspectives, and experiences. To achieve this goal, they have set standards for their platform that prioritize diversity, inclusivity, and authenticity. They have also implemented rigorous hiring practices to ensure that their team reflects the diversity of their audience and prioritizes the voices and experiences of underrepresented communities.

As Black entrepreneurs, we should strive to create businesses that reflect our values and serve our communities well. Companies like The Lip Bar, Black Girl Magic Box, and Blavity have shown that it is possible to build successful businesses while also prioritizing inclusivity, self-care, community, and supporting Black-owned businesses.

We can look at another example of a Black-owned business that has become a household name in recent years - the haircare company, Briogeo. The company's Central Demographic Model customer is women with all hair types who prioritize clean, natural ingredients in their hair products. Briogeo satisfies their customers' emotional needs for healthy, manageable hair with their use of natural ingredients and their commitment to creating products that cater to all hair types, including curly and coily hair.

In conclusion, understanding your customers' demographics and psychographics is vital to building a successful business. Set standards for your Strategic Plan that reflect your values and priorities and strive to create businesses that serve your communities well. With hard work and dedication, we can create thriving businesses that make a positive impact on our world.

CHAPTER 14
Creating a Dynamic Organizational Structure

YOUR ORGANIZATIONAL STRATEGY

All organizations are hierarchical. At each level, individuals serve those above them. An organization is, therefore, a structured entity. Without structure, it's a mob. Mobs don't create; they demolish.

Everybody desires to "get organized." But suggest an Organization Chart, and you're met with skepticism or even resistance.

"Come on," a client once snapped. "We're a small business. We don't need an Organization Chart. We need top-notch talent!"

Despite his objections, we persisted. We were aware of something he wasn't. The organizational development within an Organization Chart can profoundly impact a small business more than any other Business Development step.

Organizing Around Personalities

Most companies organize around personalities rather than functions.

That is, around individuals rather than responsibilities or accountabilities.

The outcome? Inevitable chaos.

To illustrate, let's examine Tech Titans, a new venture founded by Aisha and Zara Smith, sisters and now partners, confident in their pursuit of prosperity.

Aisha and Zara initiate their partnership by dividing the work.

When Aisha isn't coding, Zara is. When Aisha isn't pitching investors, Zara is. When Zara isn't managing social media, Aisha is.

Initially, the business runs seamlessly. The office is immaculate—Windows gleam.

Floors sparkle. Client's beam. And Aisha and Zara hustle. Alternating tasks, always alternating. Monday, Zara leads meetings. Tuesday, Aisha. Wednesday, Zara. Thursday, Aisha.

After all, they're partners, right?

If they don't do it, who will? It's only fair they share the workload.

And they continue. Business starts to boom.

Suddenly, there's more work than Aisha or Zara can handle. They need help.

Enter Marcus. A phenomenal hire. A cousin, too.

Might as well keep it in the family if you're paying someone.

Now it's Aisha, Zara, and Marcus, alternating, alternating. When Aisha isn't managing finances, Zara is. And when Zara and Aisha aren't, Marcus is.

When Zara isn't assisting a client, either Aisha or Marcus is.

Or when Aisha isn't leading meetings, Zara or Marcus is.

Things are moving. Business is thriving. Aisha, Zara, and Marcus are swamped.

Soon, Bianca joins the team. Zara's sister-in-law. An excellent addition. Diligent and eager.

Now it's Aisha, Zara, Marcus, and Bianca, alternating, alternating. When Aisha isn't managing finances, Bianca, Zara, or Marcus is. When Zara isn't supporting clients, it's Aisha, Marcus, or Bianca.

When Marcus isn't coding, it's Zara, Aisha, or Bianca.

Everyone's leading meetings, answering calls, grabbing coffee, depositing checks—alternating, alternating, alternating.

But suddenly, the software has bugs. It isn't working as it used to.

"We never had this issue before," Aisha tells Zara. Zara looks at Bianca. Bianca looks at Marcus.

Suddenly, the financials look suspicious.

"We never had this issue before," Zara tells Aisha. Aisha looks at Marcus. Marcus looks at Bianca.

And that's not all.

The office is deteriorating. Equipment vanishes. Dust accumulates on desks.

Boxes clutter workspaces. Wires tangle, and charging stations mix. Aisha, Zara, Marcus, and Bianca start bumping into each other.

Workspaces become cramped. Windows remain dirty. Floors stay unswept.

Tensions rise.

But who can speak up? What should they say? And to whom?

If everyone's doing everything, who's accountable for anything? If Aisha and Zara are partners, who's in charge? If both, what happens when Aisha instructs Marcus to do something Zara disapproves of?

When Bianca wants a break, who should she inform—Aisha? Zara? Marcus?

Who's accountable for ensuring the office is staffed?

When software glitches arise, who's accountable for fixing them?

When financials are unbalanced, who's accountable for straightening them out?

When floors need sweeping, windows need cleaning, meetings need leading, and clients need attention—who's accountable for delivering results?

What Aisha and Zara fail to comprehend is that without an Organization Chart, everything depends on luck and camaraderie, on people's personalities and mutual goodwill.

Sadly, personalities, positive vibes, goodwill, and luck aren't the sole ingredients of a successful organization; on their own, they're a recipe for chaos and catastrophe.

Organization Needs Something More

Now let's reimagine Aisha and Zara's venture, Tech Titans.

Aisha and Zara sit in their living room. They've decided to establish Tech Titans. They're excited about the prospects but understand that for it to succeed, they must approach it differently from how most people start a new business.

First, they decide to think of the business as a corporation rather than a partnership.

Instead of seeing themselves as partners, they now view themselves as shareholders.

Having both experienced unsuccessful partnerships, Aisha and Zara know that there's nothing more disastrous than a partnership gone awry, as so many do.

Unless it's a family business, that is.

Aisha and Zara already know that family businesses are even worse than partnerships.

But a partnership that's also a family business?

No. Aisha and Zara decide to do it a different way.

Sitting at the living room table, Aisha and Zara each take a blank piece of paper and print their names at the top of the page.

Beneath each name, they print "Primary Aim."

For the next hour or so, Aisha and Zara each visualize their ideal lives and write their conclusions on the page before them.

Then they spend another hour discussing what they wrote, sharing their personal dreams with each other, perhaps discovering more about each other than they had known in all their years as sisters.

The next step Aisha and Zara take is to draw a line across a blank piece of paper about a third of the way down. Above the line, they write in bold letters the word SHAREHOLDERS. They agree that this will be their role outside of the business.

Inside the business, they agree to think of themselves as EMPLOYEES from now on.

They realize this will save them a lot of trouble later on.

The next step requires some time: the creation of the Strategic Objective for Tech Titans, Inc. Aisha, and Zara enthusiastically tackle this task. Aisha agrees to research the Central Demographic Model they've tentatively chosen. How many potential buyers are in the territory where they plan to do business? Is the population growing? What's the competition like? How are tech products priced and sold? Is there a future for tech products in the territory? What's the anticipated growth of the territory? Are any zoning changes expected?

Aisha also agrees to create a questionnaire and send it to a sample of their Central Demographic Model consumers to find out how they feel they're treated by other tech companies. Simultaneously, Aisha will personally call 150 of those consumers. She'll conduct a Needs Analysis to better understand their thoughts and feelings about tech products. What do tech products mean to them? How have tech products changed their lives? If they could have any tech product at all, what would it look like? How would it feel to use it? What do they want a good tech product to do for them?

Aisha agrees to complete the research by a certain date.

Meanwhile, Zara agrees to gather the preliminary financial data needed to secure a loan from the bank—an operating pro forma and a cash flow projection for the first year of operation.

Once they collect information about consumers, competition, and pricing, Aisha and Zara will reconvene and complete their Strategic Objective, plugging in the final numbers required for the loan.

Fortune favors them. The information Aisha gathers about their Central Demographic Model, the competition, and pricing is highly encouraging.

They finalize their Strategic Objective and then embark on the task of organizational development—creating their Organization Chart.

With their Strategic Objective indicating how they'll conduct business (one location, assembling and selling tech products and tech-related accessories to a specific consumer within the territory described as South River East), Aisha and Zara agree that their Organization Chart will require the following positions:

1. President and Chief Operating Officer (COO), accountable for the overall achievement of the Strategic Objective and reporting to the SHAREHOLDERS, who include Aisha and Zara, on an equal basis.

2. Vice-President/Marketing, accountable for finding customers and discovering new ways to provide customers with the satisfaction they derive from tech products at lower cost and with greater ease, reporting to the COO.

3. Vice-President/Operations, accountable for keeping customers by delivering what Marketing promises and for discovering new ways of assembling tech products at lower cost and with greater efficiency to provide better service, reporting to the COO.

4. Vice-President/Finance, accountable for supporting both Marketing and Operations in fulfilling their accountabilities by achieving the company's profitability standards, securing capital when needed and at the best rates, and reporting to the COO.

Reporting to the Vice-President/Marketing are two positions: Sales Manager and Advertising/Research Manager. Reporting to the Vice-President/Operations are three positions: Production Manager, Service Manager, and Facilities Manager. Reporting to the Vice-President/Finance are two positions: Accounts Receivable Manager and Accounts Payable Manager.

Aisha and Zara sit back and look at the completed Organization Chart of Tech Titans, Inc., and smile. It certainly looks like a large company. The only issue is that Aisha and Zara's names will have to fill all the boxes! They're the only two employees.

But what they've effectively done is describe all the work that's going to be done in Tech Titans, Inc., when its full potential is realized.

More importantly, they have described the work that has to be done right away!

Aisha and Zara realize that there's no difference between the Tech Titans of today and the Tech Titans of tomorrow; the work is the same; only the faces will change.

The next task Aisha and Zara undertake is writing a Position Contract for each position on their Organization Chart.

Having completed the Position Contracts for the positions within their new company, Aisha and Zara, as shareholders, proceed to the most critical task of their new association: naming the people to put in the boxes.

And since there are only two of them, it becomes even more critical that they approach this task wisely and carefully if they're to avoid the errors of their past.

Once they've settled on the roles they'll each fill, they commit to their shared vision and the realization of their dream. Aisha and Zara know that this is more than just a job: it's a heartfelt commitment to the success of Tech Titans, Inc. and the fulfillment of their primary aim.

CHAPTER 15
Leading with Impact: Effective Management

You might assume that the success of a management strategy hinges on finding incredibly competent people—individuals with exceptional "people skills," management degrees, and sophisticated techniques for dealing with their team.

It doesn't.

You don't need such people, nor can you afford them. In fact, they may create more issues than they solve. What you need is a Management System. This System will become your management strategy, enabling your Franchise Avatar to produce the results you desire. The System will transform your people problems into opportunities by orchestrating management decisions and eliminating the need for such decisions wherever possible.

What Is a Management System?

A Management System is designed to produce a marketing result within your Avatar. The more automated this System is, the more effective your Franchise Avatar will be. Management Development isn't just a management tool;

it's a marketing tool. Its purpose is to create not only an efficient Avatar but an effective one—one that attracts and retains customers profitably and outperforms its competitors.

Let's examine how such a system was implemented by a nonprofit called Arts @ Large. The first time we visited Arts @ Large, we were impressed by its dedication to providing art experiences to underserved students. The organization was beautifully designed with colorful murals and student artwork displayed throughout the building, creating a welcoming and inspiring atmosphere.

As we walked in, we were greeted by a friendly staff member who explained the organization's mission and programs. They also gave us a tour of the facilities, including a performance space and several rooms for creating artwork.

Throughout our visits to Arts @ Large, we consistently experienced a high level of organization and attention to detail. The staff was dedicated to ensuring that every student had a positive and meaningful experience, from providing necessary supplies to facilitating engaging art lessons.

Curious about how Arts @ Large managed to deliver such a seamless experience, we requested a meeting with the management team. We wanted to know how they consistently produced the same results for every student.

Was it due to their highly skilled staff, an innovative incentive system, or something else entirely?

During our conversation, the manager revealed that their success came from a comprehensive Operations Manual—a series of checklists and guidelines that staff members follow to ensure the best possible experience for every student. This Management System allowed them to train new employees quickly and maintain a consistently high level of service, regardless of staff turnover.

The System covered everything from daily routines to how staff should engage with students, ensuring that the experience was personalized and tailored to individual needs. This attention to detail helped create an environment where students felt valued and heard.

For example, Arts @ Large used a data management system to keep track of each student's interests and skills, allowing them to offer relevant programs and art experiences. This level of personalization made students feel like Arts @ Large genuinely cared about their growth and development.

This Management System transformed Arts @ Large into more than just an art organization. It became a supportive community where students could connect, collaborate, and express themselves through art.

By implementing a robust and automated Management System, Arts @ Large created an efficient and effective Franchise Avatar that outperformed its competitors. The

System not only took care of the operational aspects of the organization but also ensured that each student received personalized attention, making them feel valued and supported.

In conclusion, a well-designed Management System can revolutionize your organization and set you apart from your competitors. By automating processes and paying close attention to the needs of your customers, you can create an environment where both your team and your customers can flourish.

CHAPTER 16
Cultivating a Winning Team

Small business owners often ask, "How do I get my people to do what I want?" And let me tell you, the answer differs from what you might expect.

The truth is, you can't force anyone to do anything. Instead, it would help to create an environment where your employees are motivated to do what needs to be done. You want them to feel like "doing it" is more important than "not doing it" and that "doing it" well is a way of life for them.

Let us give you an example of a hotel manager who understood this concept. When he started working for the hotel owner, he was surprised by how seriously the Boss took the hotel's operation. It wasn't just a business to him; it was an expression of who he was and what he believed in.

The owner took the time to communicate his values and ideas to the manager, which made a huge difference. As a result, the manager felt like their work reflected who they were as people, which made him respect the boss and their work.

Our advice to you is to focus on creating a workplace where your employees feel valued and understand how their work contributes to the overall mission of your business. Show them that their work is important and that they are an essential part of the team. This will help motivate them to do their best work and make your business successful.

Remember, there is no such thing as undesirable work. It's all about how you see it. You'll have a motivated and dedicated team if you can help your employees see their work as an opportunity to grow and contribute to something bigger than themselves.

Here are a few of our rules to help with developing a winning team:

Rule number one:

Figure out what you want your people to do and then try to create a game out of it. The game has to come first, and what your people do comes second if you want to be taken seriously.

Rule number two:

Never create a game for your people you're not willing to play yourself. Trust us, and they'll find out and cost you, their respect.

Rule number three:

Make sure there are specific ways to win the game without ending it. The game can never end, or it will take the life right out of your business. But victories along the way will keep your people engaged and motivated.

Rule number four:

Change the game's tactics occasionally, but never the strategy. The strategy is your game's moral foundation, but tactics must evolve to keep things fresh and exciting.

Rule number five:

Never expect the game to be self-sustaining. You must constantly remind your people about it and hold regular meetings to discuss progress and issues.

Rule number six:

The game must make sense and be based on universally verifiable truths. All logic does is give your people the rational armament to support their emotional commitment.

Rule number seven:

The game needs to be fun occasionally, but only sometimes. The thrill of playing a game well is learning how to deal with the tough parts.

And finally, rule number eight:

Steal one if you can't think of a good game. But make sure you learn it by heart and never pretend to play a game.

Remember, the game is only alive if people make it so, and we need to constantly work to keep it engaging, challenging, and fun. As African American entrepreneurs, we've seen firsthand how these rules can help you succeed. For example, look at the game-changing success of Black-owned businesses like Tushy, a company that's revolutionizing the way we think about bidets, or 4Ocean, which is tackling the issue of ocean pollution with their eco-friendly products.

So, remember these rules and keep playing the game. The journey may be challenging, but the rewards are worth it.

Let's discuss the game's logic. You might wonder, "What does that even mean?" Well, let us break it down for you.

Most people today need to get what they want. That's just the truth. They need to be fulfilled by their jobs, families, religion, government, or even themselves. And that's where the game comes in.

The game is about finding purpose, values, and worthwhile standards in your life. It's about creating something missing in today's world: a sense of community—a place where we can unite and build something great.

Now, we know what you're thinking. "But how do I create that sense of community in my business?" Well, let's give you some examples.

Take Black Girls Code, for instance. This organization is about empowering young Black girls to pursue careers in technology. They're creating a community passionate about making a difference through technology.

Or look at The Gathering Spot in Atlanta. This private club brings together entrepreneurs, creatives, and thought leaders to collaborate and connect. It's a place where you can find purpose and build relationships that will last a lifetime.

But creating a sense of community is about more than just the people you bring together. It's about the values you instill in them. Values like integrity, intention, commitment, vision, and excellence. These are the action steps that will lead you to success.

And let's be real; we're not just talking about any success. We're talking about giving your customers a sense that your business is special. It was created by special people doing something in the best possible way.

So, we want you to remember this: we can perform extraordinary acts. We can go to the moon, create computers, and build bombs that can destroy the world. So, we can only run a small business that works. And if we can do that, we'll create a community built on purpose, values, and standards. A community that's worth playing the game for.

It all starts with the logic of the game, the mental map that every successful entrepreneur needs to create. Let's look at an example of a hotel owner who created a world in which his customers experienced a profound dedication to cleanliness, beauty, and order.

But this dedication was not just about making money but a moral obligation. The owner's philosophy and ideas were communicated to his team through well-planned systems and a positive attitude. He knew that to get his team on board with his vision, he had to communicate it orderly.

The hiring process became the first and most essential medium for communicating his idea. First, it included a scripted presentation describing the idea and the attributes required for the successful candidate. Next, each applicant met individually to discuss their feelings and experiences, and the successful candidate received a scripted phone call. Finally, the first training day was designed to highlight the boss's idea and review the operations manual.

Systematizing your business need not be dehumanizing; it can be empowering. Creating an environment that allows your team to do what you want is essential. Hiring, developing, and retaining the right people requires a strategy that understands people.

But the system is only part of the solution. Without an idea worth pursuing, there can be no People Strategy. And with that idea, you can finally say, "That's where we shine!"

Let us give you an example. Imagine a baker who wants to build a successful business. She realizes that her childhood experiences, her spirit, and her passion for baking can become a philosophy for her business. She wants her business to be where the spirit is not stuffed away but celebrated. She envisions a sign above the door that says, "There will be no stuffing of the spirit here."

By creating a powerful idea and systematizing her business, she can offer true value to her employees and customers. She can create a world where her customers experience the joy of her baked goods, and her employees feel empowered to share her vision.

So, remember that the logic of the game and a powerful idea can make all the difference. Feel free to create systems that empower your team and showcase your vision. And most importantly, remember the spirit that inspired you to become an entrepreneur in the first place.

Let us break it down for you. As Breanna knows, the success of your business is all about how you do it. And by "it," we mean your business's purpose. Just like FedEx's purpose is to get your packages there overnight, your purpose should be expressed in everything you do.

For Breanna's business, Vegan Goodies Galore, her purpose is caring. How does she express caring when she answers the phone, takes a cake out of the oven, or takes money from a customer? It's all about how you do it. Every little task, every process, every bit of documentation in your operations manuals, and every bit of training at your school should reflect your purpose.

And that's what "it" is. "It" is your best way. "It" is what you believe in. "It" is why people buy from you, work for you, lend to you, and trust you. And just like we saw at the hotel we visited, the system, not just the people, sets your business apart.

But your business can soar to new heights with a management system in place combined with a well-conceived marketing system. So, make sure your "it" and your "why" is on point, your systems are in place, and watch your business thrive.

CHAPTER 17
Discovering The Art of Branding and Marketing

In the world of entrepreneurship, your marketing strategy is the key to your success. It's imperative to focus solely on your customer when developing your strategy. Forget about your dreams and visions and concentrate on what your customers want. In this digital age, with the vast amounts of data at our fingertips, there's no excuse for not knowing what your customers desire.

When developing your marketing strategy, you need to think of your customer as an irrational decision-maker. Imagine your customer standing before you, with an antenna protruding from their forehead, taking in all the sensory data around them. This sensor represents your customer's conscious mind, which absorbs information needed for making decisions, both consciously and unconsciously. The real decision-making happens in your customer's unconscious mind, where their expectations reside.

The tip of the iceberg represents the conscious thoughts and actions of a customer, such as their explicit desires, beliefs, and behaviors. These are the things that businesses can easily observe and measure through surveys, focus groups, and other forms of market research.

However, just as the iceberg is much larger beneath the surface, the subconscious desires and motivations that drive a customer's behavior are much more complex and difficult to measure. These hidden factors may include deeply held beliefs, fears, or emotional associations that the customer may not even be aware of.

To truly understand and meet the needs of their customers, businesses must be able to look beneath the surface and recognize these hidden motivations. This requires a deep understanding of human psychology, as well as the ability to gather data through more nuanced forms of research, such as observational studies or individual interviews.

By understanding the full depth of a customer's decision-making process, businesses can create products and marketing messages that speak directly to their hidden needs and motivations rather than just their conscious desires. This can lead to more successful products and more loyal customers, as the business is able to provide solutions that truly meet the needs of the whole customer, not just the tip of the iceberg.

In today's world, the first impression counts more than ever before. Whether it's a TV commercial, a print ad, social media post/ad or a sales presentation, the decision to buy or not is often made within the first few seconds or minutes. That's why you need to focus on providing the right sensory input to satisfy your customer's expectations from the get-go.

Finally, when a customer says they need to think about it, they're probably not going to think about it. In reality, the decision to buy or not was made long before you met them. Therefore, it's essential to provide the right sensory input from the start. By focusing solely on your customer and catering to their expectations, you'll create a winning marketing strategy that ensures the success of your business.

Let's talk about the two pillars of a successful marketing strategy: demographics and psychographics. If you don't know who your customer is, how can you possibly know what they want? Demographics are the science of marketplace reality. They tell you who buys. Psychographics, on the other hand, are the science of perceived marketplace reality. They tell you why certain demographic types buy for one reason while others buy for another.

Let's take Target, for example. The red bullseye logo of Target is a perfect example of how demographics and psychographics come into play. This particular shade of red has a high appeal to Target's target demographic of shoppers who value affordability and style. The color red is associated with excitement, passion, and energy, which aligns with Target's brand image of providing a fun and engaging shopping experience. If Target had chosen a different color for its logo, such as green or blue, it may not have resonated as strongly with their target audience and impacted their success in the retail industry.

Now, let's talk about the power of perception. Research shows that the navy suit is perhaps the most powerful suit a person can wear in business—immediate impact. However, if the same person wore an orange suit with an expensive white-on-white silk shirt, a green and white striped Italian silk tie, and white lizard cowboy boots, they would likely be out of business. The difference between the two men isn't in them; it's in your mind, your unconscious mind.

Perceptions are at the heart of your customer's decision-making process. If you know your customer's demographics, you can understand what those perceptions are and figure out what you must do to satisfy them and the expectations they produce. Each demographic model has a specific set of perceptions that are identifiable in advance. For example, women of a certain age, with a certain amount of education, with a certain size family, living in a certain geography buy for very specific psychographic reasons.

Psychographics is defined as the study and classification of people according to their attitudes, aspirations, and other psychological criteria, especially in market research.

Until you take marketing seriously, your avatar will continue to be a crap shoot. So, we urge you to take the time to understand your customer's demographics and psychographics and how they shape their perception. It's essential for your business's success.

Gone are the days of guessing and blind hope in business. Innovation, quantification, and strategy have taken the lead. This is not just for big companies like McDonald's, Federal Express, and Disney, but for all businesses. Your small business is more fragile than big business, so you must take marketing seriously to survive in this unforgiving age.

The challenge of our time is to learn your customer's language and communicate with them clearly. The customer is deluged with products and promises, causing confusion and indecision. You must understand what needs to be done, the essential importance of marketing to your avatar, and that your customer is less rational than you imagined.

To start, you must know who your customers are and ask them. Collecting data such as demographics, psychographics, and geographic information through questionnaires and analyzing their preferences can help you market your products effectively. Use this information to find your trading zone, a geographic perimeter within which your current customers mainly live. You can then buy a list of demographically correct people living in that area.

Marketing is not just good common sense; it's essential for small businesses to survive in today's world. So, take it seriously and start speaking your customer's language before it's too late.

CHAPTER 18
Streamlining Business with Smart Systems

In this book, we've talked a lot about systems without really defining what they are. So, let us break it down for you.

A system is a set of things, actions, ideas, and information that interact with each other and, in so doing, alter other systems. Everything is a system, from the universe to the world, to the San Francisco Bay, to the office we're sitting in, to the word processor we're using, to the cup of coffee we're drinking, to the relationship we are having—they're all systems.

In your business, there are three types of systems: Hard Systems, Soft Systems, and Information Systems.

Hard Systems are inanimate, unliving things like your computer or the colors in your office.

Soft Systems are animate, living things or ideas like you or the script for Hamlet.

Information Systems are those that provide us with information about the interaction between the other two.

Inventory control, cash flow forecasting, and sales activity summary reports are all Information Systems.

Your Business Development Plan is about innovating, quantifying, orchestrating, and integrating these three types of systems to produce a desirable result.

Let's look at Karen and Chad, two real estate agents. Karen sells ten houses a year, while Chad sells 100. What's Chad's secret? He has a selling system. He knows exactly what he needs to do at every step of the sales process, from lead generation to closing the deal. He has scripts, checklists, and templates for every part of the process. He's always improving his system and tracking his results, so he knows what's working and what's not. With his system, he can sell ten times more than Karen without working ten times harder.

Information Systems

Inventory control, cash flow forecasting, and sales activity summary reports are all Information Systems that can help you make better decisions in your business. Let's take the example of John, a barber who wants to grow his business. He tracks his revenue and expenses every month and creates a cash flow forecast for the next six months. He also tracks his inventory of products and supplies and orders new ones when he's running low. He uses a customer relationship management (CRM) system to keep track of his clients' contact.

Solutions Presentation, a crucial part of the PowerPoint Selling Process. By now, if you've done your job well, the sale is already made.

Selling is not just about closing; it's about opening up your prospect to a deeper experience of their frustration and the opportunities available to them. Through the questioning process, you can offer them remarkable new things that will make it possible for them to receive preferential treatment in the financial arena and gain control over their money and their life at a preferentially low cost.

During the Solutions Presentation, you'll provide rational armament for the emotional commitment you've established. You'll review everything you said and did during the Needs Analysis Presentation, and in great detail, you'll review your prospective customer's Financial Report. You want them to feel like this is their Financial Report, not just something that a financial expert created.

Once you've gone through the Financial Report, you'll ask your prospect which option would best serve them right now. And then you'll wait for their answer because the next person who speaks is going to make a purchase. If that's you, congratulations, you've made a sale!

To make sure you can keep making sales, you need a selling system or funnel, not just a selling person. Using the same words and reviewing the Financial Report the same way every time will ensure that you have a completely predictable technology for producing formerly unpredictable results.

To help you track the activity of your selling system, you need an Information System. This system will provide you with information about how many calls were made, how many prospects were reached, how many appointments were scheduled, confirmed, and held, how many needs analysis and solutions presentations were scheduled, confirmed, and completed, how many solutions were sold, and what the average dollar value was.

This information should be recorded on a form or a database on your computer. The Information System will tell you the rate of conversion between any two benchmarks in your selling process, which of your people are "on the system," and which ones are off it.

By calculating the cost of making a call and completing the next Benchmark in the process, you can derive the actual cost of making one sale. Without this information, you'll be left in the dark and won't know when and why you need to change.

In conclusion, hard systems, soft systems, and information systems are all crucial elements of your franchise avatar. Information is the glue that holds your systems strategy together, so make sure you have a solid information system in place. With these systems in place, you'll be able to achieve your goals and take your business to the next level.

Time is money, and there's no time left to trust a dart in the dark. In today's tech-savvy world, it's more important than ever to have a fully integrated and beautifully designed system for your business. That's where the soft systems come in.

Let us break it down for you. Your hard systems include everything visual in your business, from your shop's sign to your people's uniforms. Your information systems involve the day-to-day operations of your business, like how many pies are sold and when.

But the soft systems are where the magic happens. Every written or verbal communication with anyone who comes into contact with your business is a soft system. Your recruitment script, your shop's name, your training program, your customer brochures, your ads, and everything you say must work together to make one powerfully effective message.

And that message is your idea. The idea behind your business, the lifeblood, heart, and spirit of your business. It's what sets you apart from everyone else. And that's why it's so valuable.

So, don't just rely on your strategist's role. Embrace the power of soft systems and watch your business soar to new heights. It's fun, it's exciting, and it's the key to unlocking your business's full potential.

CHAPTER 19
Reflection: A Message for Aspiring Black Entrepreneurs

As fellow entrepreneurs, we've been reflecting on the search for purpose and meaning in our work. It's fascinating to see how even with all the technological advancements and changes in society, we're still grappling with the same questions that our predecessors faced decades ago.

We recently revisited Viktor Frankl's book, "Man's Search for Meaning," and it's striking how relevant his ideas remain today. Frankl's exploration of purpose, resilience, and the human spirit is still inspiring people worldwide, despite being published over 70 years ago.

What has changed is our approach to these questions. We often talk about success in terms of material possessions, fame, and status, but these things ultimately provide a fleeting sense of satisfaction. True meaning and purpose come from within, from a deep understanding of who we are and what we stand for.

To find this meaning, we need to challenge ourselves and step outside of our comfort zones. It's not enough to just go through the motions of our daily routine. We need to push ourselves and be willing to take risks, knowing that failure is a possibility.

We're on our own journey to discover our purpose and passion, and we know it can be a daunting process. But we also believe that it's worth it, and that each step we take towards our goals is a step closer to discovering our true potential.

So, let's embark on this journey together. Let's challenge ourselves and pursue the things that truly matter to us, regardless of how daunting they may seem, because that's what it means to be an entrepreneur - to be bold, to take risks, and to pursue our dreams with determination and resilience.

Epilogue: Reigniting the Dream for Black-Owned Businesses

This book isn't just about achieving success; it's a call to action. But before you start getting ready for battle, let us explain. It's actually a call to learning.

In today's fast-paced and ever-changing world, it can be challenging to keep up. The boundaries we once relied on no longer exist, and new rules are continuously being introduced to fill the void. Unfortunately, these new rules are often swallowed up by the vortex of change as soon as they're established.

This chaos can leave us feeling confused and unsure of what to do. However, the chaos isn't just out there in the world. It's also inside each of us. If we want to see positive changes in the world, we need to start by changing ourselves.

We're an "out there" society, always looking to fix things outside of ourselves. However, the time has come to shift our focus inward. It's time to learn how to bridge the gap between the "outside" world and the "inside" world within ourselves.

And that's where your small business comes in. Your business can be the bridge between you and the world, making both more human and productive. It's a place where you can confront your fears and learn more about yourself. A place where you can practice implementing new ideas and test your assumptions.

By doing this, you'll not only improve your business but also change your life and inspire others to do the same. So, let's take action and start learning to make a positive impact on the world.

Afterword: The Journey Begins: Stepping into Entrepreneurship

The journey of entrepreneurship is not an easy one, especially for Black entrepreneurs who have faced systemic barriers and discrimination. In "Dissecting the Black Lie," we debunked the myths that have held us back and identify the key players needed for success. Part 1 laid the foundation for the rest of the book, providing practical advice for leveling up your skills, leveraging connections, breaking chains, and developing the boss mentality.

In Part 2, we explored the urban revolution and how Black entrepreneurs can rewrite the rules to create successful businesses. We discussed designing the ultimate business blueprint and focusing on strategy over tactics.

Part 3 is where we dove deep into building a successful Black-owned business. We provided a step-by-step guide for mastering the Rise Up Business Blueprint, building a business success plan, defining your core purpose, setting bold and innovative goals, creating a dynamic organizational structure, leading with impact, cultivating a winning team, discovering the art of branding and marketing, and streamlining business with smart systems.

We ended with an epilogue that reignites the dream for Black-owned businesses and encourages aspiring entrepreneurs to take action. Our hope is that this book will serve as a guide and inspiration for Black entrepreneurs to overcome obstacles and achieve their dreams.

About The Author

The B.L.A.C.K. Masterminds is a nonprofit 501(c)(3) organization that was organized in 2020 by a group of entrepreneurs and community leaders. What started as a micro group of people connecting over Zoom to highlight Black businesses and Black issues, evolved into a hybrid resource for business owners and changemakers worldwide. Today, The B.L.A.C.K. Masterminds aims to build entrepreneurial and community leaders by facilitating and creating opportunities for shared learning that are grounded in the following four pillars of the African American community:

Entrepreneurship
Personal Development
Tech Evolution
Alliance Building

Rhonda Brown is an author, artist, mother, and entrepreneur. Rhonda has helped countless people in their writing journey to become self-published authors. She is one of the founding members and president of the non-profit The B.L.A.C.K. Masterminds.

Rhonda is co-owner of CRC Empire, where she is a digital strategist as well as a co-host of the We Got Problems Podcast.

Rhonda holds a bachelor's degree in business administration.

In her spare time, not only is she a prolific artist, Rhonda is an herbal enthusiast. Rhonda also takes time to give back by volunteering in her community.

Caliph Johnson is a husband, father, author, track coach, and entrepreneur. As a health and wellness coach, his skills and training help clients achieve their goals of living a healthier lifestyle. Caliph documented his journey to losing 100 pounds in his self-published book The Rise of The Trash Vegan.

Caliph is one of the founding members and vice president of the B.L.A.C.K. Masterminds. He is co-owner of CRC Empire and co-host of the We Got Problems Podcast.

Curtis G. Martin is an award-winning author, entrepreneur, trainer, speaker, and business owner. He was born and raised in South Central Los Angeles, where he strived to make a difference in himself and his community. He has been motivating and mentoring members of his community for over 20 years in personal development and growth. Curtis is best known for his unique training style of making courses fun while delivering valuable information.

He is one of the founding members of the non-profit The B.L.A.C.K. Masterminds, co-owner of CRC Empire LLC, and co-host of the We Got Problems Podcast.

LaCheka Phillips, a Nashville native, is a champion for entrepreneurship, giving back, and technology. With 16 years dedicated to building businesses, supporting nonprofits, and teaching digital skills, she is well-known for her leadership at the Nashville Business Incubator Center and her work with The Grammys, March of Dimes, and Leukemia Lymphoma Society. As the director of equity, inclusion, diversity, and culture at TechSoup, LaCheka continues her meaningful work aligned with her passions. She co-founded and volunteers as the Secretary for The B.L.A.C.K. Masterminds, while also co-owning CRC Empire LLC and co-hosting the We Got Problems Podcast. When not working or volunteering, she enjoys traveling, cooking, yoga, karaoke, dancing, and live music.

Made in the USA
Columbia, SC
13 July 2024

38341852R00083